WINNING

WITH

DATA

WINNING

WITH

DATA

**TRANSFORM YOUR CULTURE,
EMPOWER YOUR PEOPLE,
AND
SHAPE THE FUTURE**

TOMASZ TUNGUZ AND FRANK BIEN

Published by John Wiley & Sons, Inc., Hoboken, New Jersey
Published simultaneously in Canada

For general information about our other products and services, please contact our Customer Care Department within the United States at (800) 762-2974, outside the United States at (317) 572-3993 or fax (317) 572-4002.

Wiley publishes in a variety of print and electronic formats and by print-on-demand. Some material included with standard print versions of this book may not be included in e-books or in print-on-demand. If this book refers to media such as a CD or DVD that is not included in the version you purchased, you may download this material at http://booksupport.wiley.com. For more information about Wiley products, visit www.wiley.com.

Library of Congress Cataloging-in-Publication Data:

Names: Tunguz, Tomasz, 1981– author. | Bien, Frank, 1967– author.
Title: Winning with data : transform your culture, empower your people, and shape the future / Tomasz Tunguz and Frank Bien.
Description: Hoboken, New Jersey : Wiley, 2016. | Includes index.
Identifiers: LCCN 2016011451 | ISBN 9781119257233 (hardback) | ISBN 9781119257417 (pdf) | ISBN 9781119257394 (epub)
Subjects: LCSH: Management—Statistical methods. | Database management. | Data processing. | Data mining. | BISAC: BUSINESS & ECONOMICS / Decision-Making & Problem Solving.
Classification: LCC HD30.215 .T86 2016 | DDC 658.4/038—dc23
LC record available at https://lccn.loc.gov/2016011451

Cover Design: Wiley

Printed in the United States of America
10 9 8 7 6 5 4

Contents

Introduction

S ilicon Valley owes its existence to a Frenchman living in Boston. Born in France in 1899, Georges Doriot graduated from the University of Paris in 1920 and matriculated at the Harvard Business School in 1921. Four years after graduation, he became the assistant dean and associate professor of industrial management at Harvard.[1] Five years later, he would be promoted to full professor, in large part due to his beloved manufacturing course that graduated more than 7,000 students during his tenure through 1966. The year-long course tested the general management skills of second-year MBA students, and the final reports of students often exceeded 600 pages.[2] In *Creative Capital*, Doriot biographer Spencer E. Ante summarized his interviews of former Doriot students:

> *"His lectures were so memorable and controversial—he once lectured students on how to pick a wife—that many former students who have forgotten most of what they learned at business school still remember Doriot vividly."*[3]

A sinewy 5 feet 10 inches tall, with incisive blue eyes, a thin mustache, and a penchant for fine tobacco to stuff his iconic pipe, Doriot was highly decorated by the U.S. military. In 1940, he became a U.S. citizen to assume a military post created for him by a former student, Major General Edmund Gregory. Appointed lieutenant colonel and chief of the Military Planning Division, Doriot managed all the procurement for the U.S. Army, from trucks to uniforms to rations.

In the jungles of Southeast Asia, indigenous forces easily tracked American infantryman by their footprints. Unlike the barefooted

---

[1]McQuiston, J. T., "Molder of U.S. Businessmen." *New York Times*, June 3, 1987. Retrieved from www.nytimes.com/1987/06/03/obituaries/george-f-doriot-dies-at-87-molder-of-us-businessmen.html.

[2]Christina Pazzanese, "The Talented Georges Doriot," *Harvard Gazette*, February 24, 2015. Retrieved from http://news.harvard.edu/gazette/story/2015/02/the-talented-georges-doriot/.

[3]S. E. Ante, *Creative Capital: Georges Doriot and the Birth of Venture Capital* (Boston, MA: Harvard Business Press, 2008), 3.

natives, Americans left boot outlines as they marched through mud. So, Doriot contracted an anthropologist to develop molds of the feet of the locals and manufactured boots with these imprints on the soles. "If you ran down a muddy road you'd swear that was not an American, it was a native," remembered Lieutenant Colonel William H. McLean.[4]

In addition to these tactical advances, Doriot and his team resolved large-scale logistical problems that supplied the Allied Forces with the ammunition, nourishment, and equipment to fuel their success. Doriot was ultimately promoted to brigadier general, received the Distinguished Service Medal (the highest U.S. military metal given to a noncombatant), rose to the rank of commander of the British Empire, and was awarded the French Legion of Honor.

After the war concluded, Doriot continued to change the world. In 1959, he and three of his students from Harvard Business School founded INSEAD (Institut European d'Administration des Affairs), the preeminent business school outside the United States.

In addition, he is widely regarded as the father of venture capital. His firm, American Research and Development (ARD), led the first institutional venture capital investment of $70,000 in Digital Equipment Corporation (DEC), maker of minicomputers, in 1957. Eleven years later, DEC went public and netted more than $355 million to ARD, for a 5,000-times return and an internal rate of return (IRR) of more than 100 percent annually. Among other notable investments, Georges Doriot financed the first company of future 41st U.S. president George H. W. Bush.[5]

American Research and Development's success launched the venture capital industry. A cottage industry through the late 1990s, venture capital exploded in size and impact during the dot-com era.

In the 1980s, venture capital firms in total raised roughly $10 billion per year. During the height of the dot-com era, that figure catapulted to more than $100 billion adjusted for inflation. Since

---

[4]S. E. Ante, *Creative Capital: Georges Doriot and the Birth of Venture Capital* (Boston, MA: Harvard Business Press, 2008), 88.

[5]S. Karabell, "INSEAD at 50: The Defining Years," October 21, 2009. Retrieved from http://knowledge.insead.edu/entrepreneurship-innovation/insead-at-50-the-defining-years-1356.

then, in the course of a typical year, venture capitalists raise more than $25 billion to invest into technology, biotechnology, and other kinds of startups.

And the innovation fueled by this capital has transformed the world. FedEx, Google, Intel, Apple, Tesla, Genentech, Bed Bath and Beyond, Whole Foods, Starbucks, Uber, AirBnB: Is there an industry venture-backed startups have not yet disrupted? According to a recent study completed by Stanford researchers Ilya Strebulaev and Will Gornall, 43 percent of U.S. publicly traded companies founded after 1974 have been venture backed, accounting for 63 percent of the total U.S. stock exchange market capitalization. Further, 38 percent of American workers are employed by venture-backed businesses, including 82 percent of research and development employees.[6]

But, to hear my senior partners tell the story of the heyday of venture capital in the 1990s is to envision a completely different industry than the one we operate in today. One old-time venture capitalist recounted the ways of the bygone days: The 10 or so key members of various firms would eat lunch together on a weekly basis. Like trading baseball cards, they would swap information on the companies they'd seen and decide to invest with each other or not. The capital requirements of these startups outstripped these early funds, so they partnered to ensure the business would have enough runway to achieve success.

Of course, these syndicates competed. But even then, it was friendly. Whoever won the right to lead the series A, the first institutional round, would invite the firm that lost the opportunity to invest in the next one. However, this quid pro quo environment evaporated when the sums of money flooding the industry treated stiffer and stiffer competition from new and existing venture capital firms.

The secular increase in competition has continued over the last 20 years as the scale of technology companies has skyrocketed. Google is now worth nearly $500 billion. Facebook is worth $250 billion. And we venture capitalists chase the next one. The competition drives firms and partners within those firms to develop competitive advantages,

[6]Will Gornall and Ilya A. Strebulaev, "The Economic Impact of Venture Capital: Evidence from Public Companies," November 1, 2015, Stanford University Graduate School of Business Research Paper No. 15-55.

and in our business that means information asymmetries, and that means data and relationships. The firm that finds the next breakout company first will often win the right to invest in that business.

There are many different means for venture capital firms to establish that information asymmetry. Some of them develop unique relationships with key angel investors, individuals who invest in very early-stage companies, with just two founders and a dream. Other firms rely on strong relationships with universities and professors who refer standout students to investors. Yet others specialize, focusing on financial services technologies or consumer subscription businesses. At Redpoint, we have tried to develop an information asymmetry using data. That initiative started almost a decade ago.

I started at Redpoint, a venture capital firm headquartered on storied Sand Hill Road in Menlo Park, in 2008. During my first week, I remember receiving a thick envelope in the mail from the National Venture Capital Association (NVCA). The envelope contained the NVCA's directory, a thick tome listing all the different venture capitalists across the country. They numbered more than 5,000. Looking out of my office over the Santa Cruz Mountains, I despaired; how would I ever differentiate myself in such a competitive industry? "What would Doriot do?," I wondered.

I was very fortunate to work closely with three of the six Redpoint founders, Geoff Yang, Tim Haley, and Jeff Brody, three preeminent venture capitalists who financed billion-dollar businesses like Netflix, Juniper Networks, and HomeAway from their earliest days, and advised those businesses as they transformed huge industries. Over the next few years, they mentored me extensively, and boy did I need it.

As I started to attend board meetings with these senior partners, I began to realize how little I actually knew about startup management. Sure, I could help them with their Google advertising strategies. But founders would ask questions like "How much should I pay a VP of sales?" or "What is a reasonable cost per click on Google?" or "How fast will the business have to grow to be able to raise the next round of capital?" I was at a complete loss to answer these questions. I hoped no one in the room noted my silence.

But I knew, from my days at Google, this data must exist somewhere. So, each time a founder asked me a question about his business, be it revenue per employee benchmarks or marketing efficiencies compared to publicly traded companies, I searched for data.

Once, I found a data set containing startup IPO data dating back to the very earliest days of venture capital that Jay Ritter, a professor at the University of Florida, collected. Startups were surprisingly willing to share their internal data in surveys—anonymously, of course. So, I surveyed them. Friends working at investment banks showed me how to access the data reported by publicly traded companies.

Armed with those data sets and others, I began to answer the questions posed by founders, using the basic statistics ideas I studied in college. The data proved useful to a few of the CEOs I knew, and they asked me if they could share the data. Of course, I agreed. And one of them in particular suggested publishing the results on a blog.

I bought the tomtunguz.com domain, selected a simple blogging layout, and began to write. I jumped when 15 people read my first post. Fifteen daily readers grew to 100. One sunny summer day, I watched as my Google Analytics account reported 1,000 people had visited tomtunguz.com. In disbelief, I called my wife. All those hours spent on nights and weekends writing were finally showing some promise. That night we celebrated with some champagne.

Over the spumante, my wife asked which topics garnered the most interest. I didn't know the answer. So, I began to study the factors that attracted readers: title length, the number of subheadings, the presence of images, voice and tone, time of day to publish, and many others. I learned quite a bit.

I have 48 seconds with a reader. No pretty images, no witty title, no amount of social media validation from influencers will entice the reader to linger. Tweets sent at 8:54 to 8:59 A.M. Pacific Time generate 25 percent more views than those sent a few minutes after 9 A.M. But e-mail subscribers prefer to read content around 10 A.M., a nice midmorning break. Would e-mail readers like to read posts after lunch?, I wondered. A two-week experiment showed they most certainly did not! Open rates fell in half.

As I had done before, I published most of my findings and readers contributed experimental ideas. Over time, this iterative effort grew readership to more than 100,000 readers per month and more than 200,000 social media followers.

But what did all this content marketing ultimately create for Redpoint? A bit of a brand boost, perhaps. Could I justify investing five hours each week to this effort, especially in an industry where the most sought-after startups can raise capital in just a day or two?

At about the same time, I read Aaron Ross's book *Predictable Revenue*, which describes Salesforce's processes and tools for growing from zero to more than $6 billion in revenue. The former director of corporate sales, Aaron described Salesforce's process of finding potential customers, educating them through sales efforts, and cajoling them through the sales funnel into a satisfied, paying customer. The heart of this software process was, naturally, Salesforce's software, which catalogued the journey of all the potential buyers.

Predictable Revenue inspired me to create a sales funnel from my blog. Read by many startup founders, the blog generated leads—startups in which Redpoint might want to invest. If I could consistently and quickly identify those readers, I might be able to grow Redpoint's network of great entrepreneurs and pinpoint the next great business idea. I decided to call it Scour.

Here's how the system works. I write a blog post. That post is distributed on the web page and through e-mail, social media channels, and some other websites. This content marketing engages a broad network of people. Some of those readers elect to fortify their relationship with the content by electing to receive blog posts by e-mail.

Scour captures their e-mail address in a database. Using that e-mail address, Scour determines who the reader is by looking across the Internet: Where do they work, do they belong to a startup that could be a good fit for Redpoint, whom do we know in common, are they influential in a particular sphere like open-source software or consumer product design? This research process concludes by prioritizing a list of people to meet for us to build our network and find new startups.

Unlike the late 1990s, when the startup ecosystem encompassed perhaps 1,000 founders, today more than 4,000 technology businesses are financed each year. And, again in contrast to the previous era, today those 4,000 businesses leave digital footprints all over the Internet.

Two young computer science students might launch an experimental mobile application for iPhones. The app's success is recorded by Apple. The data is freely available for anyone to download and analyze.

As founders recruit a team, they open requisitions on job boards all over the Internet. One of the founders might decide to blog in order to build an audience of like-minded people who might eventually work for the business and also generate early demand for the product they are building. Twitter accounts, LinkedIn profiles, Facebook interactions, comments in public forums, job listings—with enough data, we have found it possible to identify very early stage startups with promise consistently.

Consequently, we have built data infrastructure to aggregate all these signals scattered across the Internet. We store them in a cloud database and continue to grow the size of that database in the hope that all this data will eventually help us find the next great business before anyone else. With this repository of information, we can experiment and explore investment hypotheses.

Some firms like First Round Capital publish their results on these kinds of trends.[7] For example, in their 10-year analysis of their investments, they found female founders outperformed their male peers by 63 percent in terms of returns generated. And founding teams with an average age less than 25 at the time of investment generate 30 percent more returns to the firm than other demographics. But the average age of all founders within the portfolio is 35. Understanding these data points is key to debunking some of the biases that lurk within the Monday partner meetings.

With this kind of data, investors can consistently make better decisions and generate more compelling returns. Again, an information asymmetry manifested in better decision making.

From its modest beginnings with American Research and Development, the venture capital industry has grown in size and sophistication. From marketing to deal sourcing and selection, data has infused every key process of a venture capital firm. And it was that data that led the Redpoint team to Looker.

---

[7]"First Round 10 Year Project," January 2016. Retrieved from http://10years.firstround.com/.

In 2012, I met Frank Bien and Lloyd Tabb, the CEO and CTO of a Santa Cruz startup, Looker. Jamie Davidson, a friend and colleague from Google, and now a partner at Redpoint, had been using Looker technology at his startup HotelTonight. Another Redpoint portfolio company, Thredup, had been using Looker to manage the operations of more than 100 employees. And they raved about it.

When Lloyd demoed Looker's technology, I fell out of my chair. I knew he had built something unique, a product that would solve the data access problem that plagued nearly every business.

The race to win the opportunity to invest in Looker was on. Over the next week, we gathered as much information on the company as possible. We called existing customers, prospective customers, former coworkers, and industry experts. They all concurred: "Looker is special."

July 8, 2013, was a Monday, a partner meeting Monday. I remember sending Frank and Lloyd access to our database a few hours before the 1:30 P.M. pitch. The database contained all the information we had aggregated on mobile startups. Lloyd told me later he modeled the data in the car, typing in the copilot seat, while Frank negotiated the conifer-curbed curves of Highway 17 from Santa Cruz to Menlo Park.

During the pitch, Lloyd showed us our data in a completely new way—the way a modern startup explores data, the way businesses create lasting information asymmetries data, the way companies win with data.

That was the beginning of our partnership.

Chapter 1

Mad Men to Math Men: The Power of the Data-Driven Culture

If we have data, let's look at data. If all we have are opinions, let's go with mine.

—Jim Barksdale, CEO of Netscape

As the television series *Mad Men* depicted, the Madison Avenue executives of the 1960s swirled scotch and smoked cigars from their Eames chairs, stoking their creative powers and developing the memorable advertising campaigns of the era. But very little of that reality remains today.

Modern marketing bears more resemblance to high-frequency stock trading than to *Mad Men*. Marketers sit in front of computers to buy and sell impressions on online advertising exchanges in a matter of milliseconds. Outputs of algorithms determine, in real time, precisely on which web page or mobile app to place an ad, precisely which variation of the ad to serve based on what the software knows about the user, and precisely how much to pay for it based on the probability the viewer will convert to a paid customer.

The paradigm shift from Mad Men to Math Men hasn't happened exclusively on Madison Avenue. This new era of marketing heralds analogous transformations in sales, human resources, and product management. No matter the role, no matter the sector, data is transforming it.

Modern sales teams employ predictive scoring technologies that crawl the web to aggregate data about potential customers and calculate the likelihood a customer will close. Each morning, sales account executives log into their customer relationship management software to a list of leads prioritized by likelihood to close. These are the new leads. The Glengarry leads.

Recruiters use data to identify the best candidates to pursue based on online profiles, blogs, social media accounts, and open-source software contributions. Product managers record the actions of users by the millisecond to understand exactly which customer journeys optimize revenue and where in the product customers exhibit confusion or drop off. Data courses through these teams by the gigabyte and supplies the essential foundation for decision making throughout the organization.

As novelist William Gibson said, "The future is already here—it's just not very evenly distributed."[1] A small number of companies have restructured themselves, their hiring practices, their internal processes, their data systems, and their cultures to seize the opportunity provided by data. And they are winning because of it. They exemplify the future. Inevitably, these techniques will diffuse through industry until everyone remaining employs them.

With this book, we'll illuminate how forward-thinking businesses already operate in the future, and outline how we have seen others evolve their businesses, their technology, and their cultures to win with data.

Operationalizing Data: Uber's Competitive Weapon

Who among us does not say that data is the lifeblood of their company? The largest hoteling company [AirBnB] owns no hotel rooms. The largest taxi company [Uber] owns no taxis.
                                            —Ash Ashutosh, CEO of Actifio

At their core, the best data-driven companies operationalize data. Instead of regarding data as a retrospective report card of a team's performance, data informs the actions of each employee

---

[1]William Gibson, "The Science in Science Fiction," *Talk of the Nation*, NPR, November 30, 1999.

every morning and every evening. From harnessing customer survey responses to evaluating loan applications, these Math Men and Women are transforming every industry and every function.

As Ash Ashutosh said, the biggest transportation and lodging companies own no infrastructure. Instead, they manage data better than anyone else. Just four years after Uber was founded, its San Francisco revenues totaled more than three times all the revenues of all the taxi cab companies in the city. Two years later, the Yellow Cab Cooperative, which has operated the largest fleet of taxis in San Francisco for decades, filed for bankruptcy.

Among many innovations, Uber brought data to the taxi industry. Using historical data, Uber advises drivers to be in certain hotspots during certain times of day to maximize their revenue because customers tell them with the push of a button where to be. Uber matches the closest driver with the customer to minimize wait time and maximize driver utilization and earnings.

In contrast, disconnected Yellow Cab drivers listen to a coffee-fueled, fast-talking dispatcher relaying telephone call requests by radio. Individual drivers claim passenger pickups by responding over the CB, even if they are the furthest cab from the customer. "How long until the taxi arrives?"

Dispatchers can handle only one request at a time, serially. In rush hour, potential passengers redial after hearing a busy tone. Let too much time elapse coming from the other side of town and your passenger has already jumped into an Uber. For the Yellow Cab driver, the gas, time, and effort are all wasted because of an information asymmetry. In comparison to Uber, Yellow Cab drivers are driving blind to the demand of the city, and Yellow Cab customers are blind to the supply of taxi cabs.

Uber changes its pricing as a function of demand, telling drivers when it makes sense to start and stop working. Surge pricing, though controversial, establishes a true market for taxi services. Yellow Cab drivers don't know the best hours to work and prices are fixed regardless of demand.

Data improves more than the marketplace efficiency. Uber employs drivers based on their customer satisfaction data provided by consumers. Drivers who score below a 4.4 on a 5.0 scale risk "deactivation"—inability to access Uber's passenger base. Meanwhile, the Yellow Cab company maintains an average Yelp review of less than 1.5 stars out of 5.

The data teams that optimize Uber driver locations, maximize revenue for drivers, and drive customer satisfaction operate on a different plane from the management of the Yellow Cab company. Blind, Yellow Cab drivers are completely outgunned in the competitive transportation market. They don't have what it takes to compete: data.

But the Uber phenomenon isn't just a revolution in the back office. It's also about a new generation of taxi drivers, who operate their own businesses in a radically different way. What cabbie in the 1990s could have dreamed that upon waking early in the morning, a mobile phone would suggest there's more money to be made in the financial district of San Francisco than at the airport? But the millennial driver knows the data is attainable: It's just a search query or text message away. This is the fundamental, secular discontinuity that data engenders.

The Era of Instant Data: You Better Get Yourself Together

Instant Karma's gonna get you
Gonna knock you right on the head
You better get yourself together
Pretty soon you're gonna be dead

—John Lennon

The demand for instant data will increase inexorably. Like Uber drivers seeking a passenger at this very moment, we expect answers instantly. If you're making Baked Alaska for company tonight, and you've forgotten the ratio of sugar to egg whites in the meringue that houses the ice cream, your phone will answer the question in just a few seconds.

Where is Priceline stock trading? Where do the San Francisco Giants stand in this year's pennant race? When hiring a litigation attorney, what are the key questions to ask? Are there any grammatically sound sentences in English where every word starts with the same letter?

All of these questions are instantly answerable. These are the types of questions we ask at the dinner table or when sharing a drink with a friend at a bar, and answer in a few seconds with a search query on a phone.

Because of this new instant access to just about every kind of information, we expect the same instantaneity of answers at work. Why did our sales team outperform last quarter? Which of my clients are paying the most? Does this marketing campaign acquire customers more efficiently than the others? Should we launch our product in Japan in December?

In most companies, these questions require days or weeks to answer. Consequently, data is a historical tool, a useful rearview mirror to the well-managed business. It's a lens through which we can understand what happened in the past. And, if we're lucky, it can help us understand a little bit about why the past unfolded in a particular way.

But this level of analysis pales in comparison with the practices of best-in-class companies that operationalize their data. These are businesses that use the morning's purchasing data to inform which merchandise sits on the shelves in the afternoon.

What have those companies done to access instant data? First, they've changed the way they manage themselves, their teams, and their companies; they've changed how they run meetings, how they make decisions, and how they collaborate. Employees are data literate: They understand how to access the data they need, how to analyze it, and how to communicate it well.

Second, these companies have developed functional data supply chains that send insight to the people who need it. A data supply chain comprises all the people, software, and processes related to data as it's generated, stored, and accessed. While most of us think of data as the figures in an Excel spreadsheet or a beautiful bar chart, these simple formats often hide the complexity required to produce them.

The simple Excel spreadsheet hides a churning sea of data, coursing through the company's databases, that must be synthesized and harmonized to create a single, accurate view of the truth. A data infrastructure that permits easy, instant access to answers to business questions by anyone in the company is the second step.

Third, these businesses create a data dictionary, a common language of metrics used by the company. When sales and marketing refer to a lead, the definition of a lead must be consistent across both teams. Often, different teams within a company define metrics in unique ways. Though convenient for the individual team, this approach creates confusion, inconsistency, and consternation. Robust data pipelines ensure a universal language across the company.

This combination of bottoms-up data literacy, top-down data infrastructure, and a single metrics lexicon has transformed many businesses. Google was one of the first to empower its employees with unfettered access to critical business data. Consequently, Google employees were able to leverage the company's enormous reach and resources to develop breakthrough products.

That innovation in the early 2000s cascaded through many other large and small companies, including Facebook, LinkedIn, Zendesk, and others. Above all, these companies architected data supply chains that enable their employees to extract the insights they needed to advance the company's causes. Unfortunately, most businesses still operate with outdated supply chains buckling under the strain of data demand. You better get your data together, or pretty soon you're gonna be dead.

Data Supply Chains: Buckling Under the Load

Slow data is caused by an inefficient supply chain. Today's data supply chains suffer from a fundamental flaw in their architecture: The number of people seeking data dwarfs the number of people supplying data. The taxi dispatcher relaying passenger pickups by phone serves scores of drivers, each seeking their next fare. In many companies, this ratio may be much greater than 100:1. Is it any surprise that the data analyst team is seen as an enormous bottleneck, a chokepoint for the organization?

In the past, this flawed architecture functioned because most companies had a relatively small amount of data, most of it created by humans, and the competition wasn't using data for a competitive advantage. Without a substantial corpus of data to interrogate, only a handful of executives asked questions of their company's data, limiting the total number of requests. Most of the time, these requests were financial in nature and managed by the CFO and his organization.

But the amount of data that companies store today has exploded. According to IDC, from 2013 to 2020, the digital universe will grow by a factor of 10, from 4.4 trillion to 44 trillion gigabytes. It more than doubles every two years. This supernova of data contains insights relevant for every person within an organization.

Today, computers generate data at rates that far outstrip humans. Facebook records more than 600 petabytes of data daily on its users, almost all of it generated by computers. This trend isn't constrained to social networks. For example, Marketo, Eloqua, Pardot, and Hubspot pioneered the marketing automation software category not more than 10 years ago. These tools help B2B (business-to-business) marketers optimize demand-generation programs and prioritize leads. Market automation software snares data on website visitors to answer typical marketing questions: What content are they reading? How frequently are they visiting the site? What are the best messages to generate more leads?

Now that we're collecting all this data, we expect instant answers from it. In larger companies, the burden for answers rests on the shoulders of the data team. These scarce data analysts must process an ever-lengthening queue of work. Each request carries with it a unique set of intricacies. Perhaps the query involves a new data set, or a new type of data analysis, or a new visualization. And maybe the requesters of the data weren't quite sure what they were asking at the outset, so they revise the requested analysis, adding again to the workload and slowing processing time for everyone else. Rarely do most employees understand the complexity of their requests: the number of steps, the turnaround time, or the number of players required to answer their questions.

For smaller companies, there's often a cadre of people, perhaps just one or two, who understand how to pull data from databases, something they do in their spare time or after hours as favors to colleagues. Quickly, the volume and sophistication of these requests overwhelms the moonlighters, who can't possibly support the demand.

To extract value from these mountains of ones and zeros, companies can no longer rely on a small coterie of radio dispatchers broadcasting outdated information to their employees. Nor can they simply supply stronger coffee so dispatchers speak faster. The external competitive pressures and internal demand for accurate and relevant data are too great.

In both cases, the end result is the same. The data infrastructure simply cannot satisfy the demands of data consumers within the organization. Starved for insight, employees substitute instinct, gut, back-of-the-envelope calculations, estimates, and other short-circuited research to decide.

The data dispatcher system won't scale to meet these new needs. More dispatchers, more radios, more caffeine won't solve the problem. A new data supply chain must be built.

Management by Opinion: The Illusion of Knowledge

The greatest enemy of knowledge is not ignorance, it is the illusion of knowledge.

—Stephen Hawking

Like Yellow Cab, most companies manage with a few dispatchers. The constraints of the data supply chain engender inequality. Limited bandwidth forces the company to prioritize only the most important data; for most businesses, that means data requested by the C-suite. Everyone else must resign themselves to deciding using opinion, gut, and conjecture.

This is the worst outcome of all. Paraphrasing Stephen Hawking, the greatest enemy of business progress is the illusion of knowledge. If we make decisions based on guesses or opinions or word of mouth, we are all just wasting time, like a taxi driver wandering the city streets in search of the next fare. *Perhaps I should drive to the financial district. I've had luck there before. My friends tell me the airport should be busy this weekend.*

How should a team dispel the illusion of knowledge? Dominic Orr, former CEO of Aruba Networks, insists on brutal intellectual honesty in his management teams. "We focus on collecting as many facts as quickly as we can, and then we decide on the best, but not necessarily the perfect, solution. Think Socratic method at the speed of light."[2] Insisting on brutal intellectual honesty within a company or a team demands great trust between team members and ensures the best decision is consistently made, for the right reasons. Not politics, not gut, nothing but informed decisions.

Imagine a world where data is put into the hands of the people who need it, when they need it, not just for Uber drivers, but for every team in every company. This is data democratization, the beautiful vision of supplying employees with self-service access to the insights they need to maximize their effectiveness. This is the world of the most innovative companies today: technology companies like Uber, Google, Facebook, and many others who have re-architected their data supply chains to empower their people to move quickly and intelligently.

Modern data infrastructure is necessary but insufficient for a company to become data-driven. A cutting-edge data supply chain that's unused is just as worthless as a nonexistent one. Culture is the key ingredient to ensuring data investments achieve their potential.

The core values of a company define its culture. The disruptive companies described in this book prize curiosity, collaboration, and a desire to use data for decisions. Data must be part of every important discussion and decision.

These values start when hiring. At Google, the recruiting teams evaluate candidates on several attributes, most notably Googliness, an eponymous characteristic of the company. Googliness refers to many things, most notably intellectual curiosity: the desire to ask questions and understand why. Google hires only candidates who exhibit googliness.

To support these curious minds, Facebook and Zendesk, like Google, employ data teams. These data teams architect data systems, educate employees to use them, tutor teams on correct analytical methods, and assist individuals when crafting arguments using data. In addition, these data teams collaborate across all the departments of these businesses to design, maintain, and circulate a data dictionary, a common lexicon of metrics used across the business.

---

[2]Cathy Olofson, "So Many Decisions, So Little Time," *Fast Company*, September 30, 1999.

By inculcating a common set of values, offering the tools and education, and creating a common language, data teams within these businesses empower their colleagues to decide how to advance the company using data, instead of opinions.

At their core, data teams disperse the fog of ignorance within a company. They democratize data access and disseminate knowledge across a business. And the business evolves from responding to a dispatcher's radio comments to deciding with a real-time, bird's-eye view of all the customers in a city seeking a taxi.

Our Vantage Points

Once one company within a sector begins to win with data, as Uber has, the only competitive response from its peers will be the development, deployment, and use of data at scale. We have no doubt that this approach to data will cascade into every position in every business in every industry, because we have seen it firsthand.

TOM TUNGUZ, PARTNER AT REDPOINT

I first learned about the value of data sets at Google. I started in the AdSense Operations team, which managed the accounts of large web publishers who ran Google's ads on their web pages. About a year later, I transferred into the product management team at Google and began to work with teams of marketers, engineers, and user-experience researchers to build new products. Over the next 24 months, we built products to monetize some of the largest social networks in the world by ingesting anonymized data about users to improve our ad targeting.

We also localized AdSense into many new languages. Statistics played a key role in interpreting other languages. In English, sentences contain spaces between words; not so in Chinese. Further complicating things for computers trying to understand Chinese text, the Chinese language uses compound words frequently. Cell phone is *shšují* (手机), which are the characters for "hand" and "machine." A lobster is *lóngxiā* (龙虾), or "dragon shrimp." And a turkey is *huǒ jī* (火鸡), meaning "fire chicken." Engineers used complex statistics to infer the meaning of the author and to target ads better. A misinterpretation of the content could lead to hilarious results.

After Google, I joined Redpoint, a venture capital firm with a long history of investing in breakthrough companies like Netflix, Sonos, Stripe, and Zendesk, among many others, at the very earliest stages. At Redpoint, we've invested heavily in using data to help us find great companies, even if they might be just a few people typing away in an apartment in San Francisco.

Startups today leave footprints all over the Internet. Two cofounders will meet on LinkedIn and begin to chat with each other on Twitter. They will post job listings on hiring boards all over the web. They might launch an application on the Apple App Store. We continue to build data tools to pick up those bread crumbs, each a clue about what might be the next billion-dollar business.

In addition, we benchmark companies constantly, comparing growth rates, marketing efficiency, word-of-mouth vitality, and many other metrics. This rich database informs our investment decisions. We also use this data to provide targets for our portfolio companies, the businesses we invest in.

Last, we have developed a metrics-driven content market-ing strategy to build our brand with hundreds of thousands of entrepreneurs all over the world. Ten years ago, the world of venture capital could have been called a cottage business: friends in different firms trading deals over a fancy lunch. Today, venture capital part-nerships invest heavily in their data infrastructures to gain a small edge, the iota of information asymmetry that might lead to the next multi-billion-dollar giant.

Our experience building internal data tools and engendering a data-centric culture at Redpoint helps us invest in companies building next-generation data technologies. In 2012, we were lucky to meet Frank and the team, and we were amazed by the Looker product, especially when they connected a Looker instance to our internal data sets and we could analyze the trends like never before. A few days later, we shook hands on a partnership. Since then, Looker has become the fastest-growing business intelligence (BI) company of the past 20 years.

FRANK BIEN, CEO OF LOOKER

For 20 years, I have worked in the world of databases, including Greenplum, a maker of high-performance analytics databases acquired by EMC, Dell, and Intraspect Software.

When the whole idea of Big Data emerged, around 2002 and 2003, I was excited to see what would happen. Big Data gave us a new infrastructure. It gave us systems that could store everything. And it engendered data-mining pursuits, predictive queries about how much customers might buy or how deep a discount would generate more revenue.

But I was painfully aware that nobody had cracked the code on how to build on top of big data in such a way that it was usable by business people. They were still building BI tools for different kinds of databases. Companies were installing these giant machines and collecting massive amounts of data, and then doing trivia questions that had no business value. I knew that if people had a new kind of tool to see into all their data, they could change how their business operated, and everybody could be like a Google. Even a small company could make better-informed decisions, driven by what they understood to be true.

When I met Lloyd Tabb, the founder of Looker, I was impressed with the company's customers. I could see that businesses, *some* businesses, were ready to do data in that new way. The early Looker customers were the most innovative of the innovative, San Francisco startups and Silicon Valley–funded companies. CEOs, data teams, and everyone in between were deeply interested in data. They didn't want the old BI tools. They didn't want to work in PowerPoint. They didn't want the pictures. They wanted to get inside.

That's when, and why, I joined Looker. With Looker, the relationship these groundbreaking companies had with data was fundamentally different, just like the web browser fundamentally changed our relationship to information. Together, they're creating a "Give me the proof" kind of business culture that is driving the success of their businesses. Nerds have become the new mainstream. They don't want the toys. They're ready for a real toolbox. That shift has allowed Looker to succeed.

The results speak for themselves: From business users in marketing to PhD-level data scientists, Looker users get hooked on data.

We started out as a technical product aimed at data people who wanted code, fast and agile. But when we empowered the data people to be creative, curating data for the rest of the company, rather than answering one-off questions, something else happened. We noticed that business users started asking more questions. When they finally had access to everything, not just to tidbits, they went crazy. One question would lead to another. They started asking a hundred questions, and they started using data to evaluate, explain, and defend their decisions. What they learn has made them, and their businesses, smarter.

In this book, we hope to share what we both have learned within our own companies and within exceptional startups and monoliths about how to transform a company with data.

Chapter 2

Four Problems with Data Today: Breadlines, Obscurity, Fragmentation, and Brawls

Data Breadlines for the Data-Poor

Charles Louis Fleischmann, a Czech educated in Budapest, Vienna, and Prague, emigrated to the United States in 1865 with his brother Max. Upon arriving in Ohio, they were both immediately disappointed by the quality of local bread. Enterprising men, the Fleischmann brothers partnered with a local financier named James Gaff to found the Fleischmann Yeast Company in 1868. They spent the next two years producing and patenting a compressed yeast cake that transformed baking in America.

In addition to their ubiquitous yeast, the Fleischmanns were also famous for their generosity. In the 1880s, the Vienna Model Bakery of New York started a tradition. Each night, they doled out all the unsold bread to the poor, creating the first breadline. Eventually, the line grew to 500 people long.[1] Five decades later, long breadlines became a vivid artifact of the Great Depression, when thousands of men, unable to provide for themselves or their families, lined up to receive bread.

When I think about the behavior of many business people today, I imagine a breadline. These employees are the data-poor, waiting around at the end of the day on the data breadline. The overtaxed

---

[1] "A 10th Street Bakery Coins the 'Breadline," *Ephemeral New York*, June 13 2011. Retrieved from https://ephemeralnewyork.wordpress.com/2011/06/13/a-10th-street-bakery-coins-the-term-breadline/.

data analyst team prioritizes work for the company executives, and everyone else must be served later. An employee might have a hundred different questions about his job. How satisfied are my customers? How efficient is our sales process? How is my marketing campaign faring?

These data breadlines cause three problems present in most teams and businesses today. First, employees must wait quite a while to receive the data they need to decide how to move forward, slowing the progress of the company. Second, these protracted wait times abrade the patience of teams and encourage teams to decide without data. Third, data breadlines inhibit the data team from achieving its full potential.

Why does the data breadline keep lengthening? Since the data team has many mouths to feed, most people will have to satisfy themselves with just one or two answers to key questions. But demand for data from every part of the company is insatiable. When faced with data shortages and analysis backlogs that range from several days to several weeks, data teams hire more analysts to increase throughput. More bakeries means higher throughput, but no matter how large the team, there will always be more questions than bread, leaving employees to wait on the breadline.

Today's employees are asking more questions, and they expect instant answers. To be truly data-driven, a business must enable all of its employees to ask and answer 80, 90, or even 100 percent of their questions quickly, an impossible proposition for existing data supply chain architectures.

Unfortunately, there's a worse consequence to long data breadlines: People drop out. As employees experience long latencies for their initial data requests, they quickly learn not to ask for data, because there's no expectation it will arrive in time to be of value. So, they stop posing interesting questions. Or worse, they guess the answer. For these employees, the data architecture may as well not exist. This phenomenon causes the data breadline problem to appear smaller than it truly is.

In these trying circumstances, data consumers aren't the only ones who suffer. Data analysts struggle to deploy their skills usefully. These highly trained individuals, many of whom are statisticians, were enlisted to perform deep business analyses, including linear regressions, clustering, and predictive modeling, to help company leaders make the right strategic decisions. But because they're inundated performing basic reporting to meet the growing hunger for data, they never have bandwidth to perform the meaningful research they were trained and hired to fulfill. Instead of creating insight from data and building predictive models, these statisticians are summing and dividing simple figures.

Data breadlines suffocate organizations. Teams don't receive timely answers to their questions, or any answers at all. Data analysts don't leverage their expertise to its fullest extent. Teams make uninformed decisions. Consequently, the company never realizes the true value of its investments in people or data.

Data Obscurity: The Failure of the Card Catalog

Once an employee has been patient enough to reach the front of the data breadline, he gets to ask the data analyst team to help him answer his question. The conversation bears more than a passing resemblance to one between a third-grade student and a librarian.

When I was in grade school, like many other students in America, I was taught the Dewey decimal system, a scale from 0 to 1,000, under which every book in the universe can be categorized. Created by Melvin Dewey in 1876 and totaling 314 pages with 10,000 index entries, the decimal system took the U.S. libraries by storm. By 1927, 96 percent of the libraries studied were using Dewey's system. And it's still in use today after 23 revisions.[2]

There's no more concrete manifestation of the Dewey decimal system than the beloved card catalog, a wooden box housing a constellation of little drawers with thousands of index cards, each referring to a book on a shelf in the library.

---

[2]Dewey Decimal Classification, n.d. Retrieved January 28, 2016, from https://en.wikipedia.org/wiki/Dewey_Decimal_Classification.

To research a paper, as I did in third grade, you might pay a visit to the librarian at your local library and ask where the books on Charles Lindbergh and aviation might be. After consulting the card catalog, the librarian will tell you that books on early aviation would be found at Dewey location 387.7 and Charles Lindbergh's biography would be in 920. But before you go, you should know that nonfiction books are organized by the Dewey number while the biographies are organized by the last name of the person.

At that moment, you would feel exactly like most employees do when they ask for data guidance: baffled. Why are there two different locations for these books and, within each, two systems for organizing the data?

But within companies, there aren't two locations for data. There could be hundreds. Some data sets are in use by the sales team, others by the engineering team. Worse, there is no single card catalog for a company's data. In fact, corporate data bears much more resemblance to a huge pile of card catalog index cards scattered across the library floor. There is no map or organization of any of the data. Who created this data set? Who manages it? What does it contain?

In fact, 60 percent of companies surveyed by the *The Economist* cited disorganized data as the key reason for trailing peers in their use of data.[3] So, employees must sift through the morass of 3 × 5-inch index cards, hoping to stumble upon the right one quickly.

Just as the librarian is an essential translator from the arcane syntax of the Dewey decimal system into English, a few select data engineers understand how the labyrinths of data are organized. Companies maintain thousands of databases, each with hundreds of tables and billions of individual data points. In addition to producing data, the already overloaded data teams must translate the panoply of figures into something more digestible for the rest of the company, because with data, nuances matter.

Even expert data analysts lose their bearings sometimes, which results in slow response times and inaccurate responses to queries. Both serve to erode the company's confidence in their data.

---

[3] *The Economist* Intelligence Unit, "Decisive Action: How Businesses Make Decisions and How They Could Do It Better," n.d. Retrieved January 29, 2016, from www.economistinsights.com/sites/default/files/Decisive Action - How businesses make decisions.pdf.

Rogue Databases and Analysts: The Data Fragmentation Problem

One of the reasons for failure is that the knowledge-creating system,
the method by which humans collectively learn and by which insti-
tutions improve themselves, is deeply fragmented.

—Peter Senge and Daniel Kim

Suppose, by some miracle, you had found Charles Lindbergh's biography in the library. Leafing through its pages, you might have learned that Lindbergh and Amelia Earhart worked together to promote the first commercial passenger airline service, called Transcontinental Air Transport.

Right then, curiosity might compel you to learn about Amelia Earhart's last voyage on her Lockheed Electra plane. You would have to return to the librarian and start again. But this time, you would face additional problems: Which of the books on her last voyage is the most thorough one? Does the library have the latest books with the new discoveries? Who is the expert on the topic? There is no way to tell which is the most accurate source.

The same challenge arises in companies. Overly delayed by the strapped data team and unable to access the data they need from the data supply chain, enterprising individual teams create their own rogue databases. These shadow data analysts pull data from all over the company and surreptitiously stuff it into database servers under their desks.

I was one of those shadow data analysts. At Google, I kept a server underneath my desk and named it after a colleague's dog, an innocuous and playful Yorkshire terrier named Lucas.

Our team sold new customers, managed their accounts, and helped them grow their revenues using Google's ad products. A small group of us worked with social networks like MySpace, LinkedIn, and Facebook, which were nascent at the time. During this era, Google battled fiercely with Yahoo's competing product, the Yahoo Publishing Network. When I joined AdSense, the team was concentrating on winning the market share war with Yahoo. But we hadn't any idea how much share we had compared to Yahoo.

Since Google crawls most of the Internet, we could see which web pages ran Google ads and which ran Yahoo ads. But all that information resided within the databases of the Google search index team. The breadline wasn't just too long; it was closed to AdSense.

So, I partnered with a friend on the engineering team at Google to build a competitive tracking tool that used the output of the Google crawler to show us our relative market share each day. More importantly, this analysis showed us the key customers who were trailing Yahoo's products, enabling us to prioritize them in our acquisition efforts.

We stored all this essential information in the Lucas server, unbeknownst to anyone else inside of Google except our managers. We were rogue database operators. No one validated our data, and no one communicated to us when there was a change to the underlying crawl that we were mining to perform our analysis.

Duplicated, isolated rogue datasets create fragment data in silos like the one little server I kept at Google. They quickly fall out of date, leading to large and small inaccuracies, which can spread misinformation throughout a company. After a few months, it's almost impossible to know anything about the quality of the data. Which Excel spreadsheet is the latest? Are there any errors in the analysis? Who built this model? What does this column mean? Has anyone altered the data in the data set somewhere along the way? Has this data set been extracted from the official data set or from some unauthorized database?

This problem doesn't just happen at the end of a data pipeline. Most data pipelines process data piecemeal. The operations team dumps a large file into a folder. Next, the data analyst team manipulates the data to suit the data query, using a new set of tools, and sends this file to the person asking for the data, who uses another set of tools to visualize and package the information for an executive presentation.

Segmented data pipelines suffer from a fatal flaw: error can be introduced at any stage. A file could be truncated when the operations team passes the data to the analyst team. The data analyst team might use an old definition of customer lifetime value. And an overly ambitious product manager might alter the data just slightly to make it look a bit more positive than it actually is. With this kind of siloed pipeline, there is no way to track how errors happen, when they happen, or who committed them. In fact, the error may never be noticed.

These are just a handful of problems that plague brittle systems that silo data. Take the example of a basic spreadsheet exported from a database. As soon as the export takes place, as soon as the data is transferred from the data pipeline system into the file, the data is out of date, a manifest risk for misinforming customers, vendors, partners, colleagues, or executives across the organization.

This is also true for unmaintained data warehouses and books. Without centralizing the data, all in one place, inaccurate and disputable data is inevitable.

Data Brawls: When Miscommunication Devolves into Arguments

Data fragmentation has another insidious consequence. It incites data brawls, where people shout, yell, and labor over figures that just don't seem to align and that point to diametrically different conclusions.

Imagine two well-meaning teams, a sales team and a marketing team, both planning next year's budget. They share an objective: to exceed the company's bookings plan. Each team independently develops a plan, using metrics like customer lifetime value, cost of customer acquisition, payback period, sales cycle length, and average contract value.

When the two teams come together to share their plans, they present radically different approaches based on radically different data. And a data brawl breaks out. Who is right? How did you reach that conclusion? That number isn't right! Where did you get that data?

So what went wrong? Each team requested data separately. Neither team collaborated with the data team to define all of these key metrics in one way across the organization. Each team built their plans separately using different data. The sales team projects sales cycles that are 15 percent shorter than the marketing team's projections because they used different dates to demarcate the time a customer enters the sales funnel. The marketing team suggests a

30 percent smaller lead requirement because they measure lead quality using unqualified e-mail sign-ups while the sales team insists on using leads that have been screened over the telephone.

When there's no consistency in the data among teams, no one can trust each other's point of view. So meetings like this devolve into brawls, with people arguing about data accuracy, the definition of shared metrics, and the underlying sources of their two conflicting conclusions.

We've seen this problem at hundreds of companies and the source of the problem is always the same: There's no single definition of each metric the company uses, and there's no canonical place to access that data. Without a universal lexicon, confusion is inevitable and conflict unavoidable.

Chapter 3

Business Intelligence: How We Got Here

Business Intelligence Is Born: The First Query

Business intelligence (BI) processes and systems trace their lineage to a 1958 paper written by Hans Peter Luhn, an IBM researcher. Luhn performed the first business intelligence query.

> Mr. Luhn, in a demonstration, took a 2,326-word article on hormones of the nervous system from *The Scientific American*, inserted it in the form of magnetic tape into an I.B.M. computer, and pushed a button. Three minutes later, the machine's automatic typewriter typed four sentences giving the gist of the article, of which the machine had made an abstract. Mr. Luhn thus showed, in practice, how a machine could do in three minutes what would have taken a technician at least half an hour's hard work.[1]

In his paper "A Business Intelligence System," Luhn described the flow of business information, from photo prints and transcriptions on magnetic tape to auto-recording and auto-abstracting, all the way through to considering what is known, who needs to know, and who needs what and communicating the appropriate information via any number of then-available media. Luhn waxed on about a problem still unsolved more than 70 years after the publication of his paper: "One of the most crucial problems in communication is that of channeling a given item of information to those who need to know it."

---

[1]"Hans Peter Luhn, Mentor, 68, Dies," *New York Times*, August 20, 1964. Retrieved from www.nytimes.com/1964/08/20/hans-peter-luhn-mentor-68-dies.html?_r=0.

Luhn proposed surfacing relevant data to employees by desk printers, telephones, and photocopies. Here's how it worked:

> Each document entering the system ... is assigned a serial number and is photographically reproduced on some medium such as microfilm.... Under the supervision of an experienced librarian the process of information retrieval is performed in the following way. A [person] telephones the librarian and states the information wanted. The librarian will then interpret the inquiry and will solicit sufficient background information from the [person] in order to provide a document similar in format to that of documents normally entering the system.[2]

Although the underlying technologies have changed, most data supply chains operate in exactly the same way today as they did in 1958. A user asks a data engineer to understand his business problem, translate that into the language of the business intelligence system, and return a data set.

This supply chain architecture posits one assumption that is no longer true: that storage of vast volumes of data is expensive.

Databases for the Masses: Oracle Commercializes Codd's Invention

Most companies store data in databases, a technology invented in 1970 by another IBM employee named Edgar Codd. Codd's solution stored data in an array of columns and rows, just like a giant Excel spreadsheet, and provided a way for computers to search large amounts of the data quickly. Each cell within the database could be uniquely identified by an address composed of its column and row, for example "F23." Of course, modern databases can store terabytes of data, compared with just a few tens of thousands of rows for Microsoft Excel.

While IBM invented the database, Larry Ellison's Oracle Corporation commercialized the technology and reshaped the information technology industry along with it. Ellison cofounded Oracle in 1977

---

[2]Hans Peter Luhn, "A Business Intelligence System," *IBM Journal*, October 1958, 314–319.

with Bob Miner and Ed Oates. Initially called Software Development Laboratories, the company changed its name to Relational Software in 1979, before finally dubbing itself Oracle Systems Corporation in 1982.

One year after the founding of the company, Ellison's team completed the first version of an Oracle database. However, the company didn't sell a single copy, opting instead to work for another year to build a second version of the software. Ellison and his cofounders believed that no customer would purchase the first version of a database. It simply hadn't yet proven its stability and its ability to accurately retain data.

Upon completing version 2, Oracle closed its first customer, Wright-Patterson Air Force Base, one of the most complex bases operated by the United States Air Force. Located in Ohio, Wright-Patterson was the site of the Wright Brothers' original flight tests and continues to host many aerial test flights, including world record–setting altitude tests. It's also the headquarters for the National Air and Space Intelligence Center (NASIC), an Air Force unit that evaluates and studies foreign space weapons and systems.

Over the following four years, Oracle released three more versions of its software, culminating with version 5.1 in 1986. That same year, the company filed to go public and completed its IPO with a revenue of $55 million. Today, Oracle is the second-largest enterprise software company in the world, with a revenue of $38 billion and a market cap approaching $200 billion. At the core of all Oracle products is its first database, using the same technology that Edgar Codd invented at IBM.

Oracle has since become the dominant developer of databases by virtue of its powerful technology, and also its extremely high prices. Though Oracle's pricing structure is complex, customers pay thousands to tens of thousands of dollars per year to store a single terabyte of data. In addition, customers must pay millions of dollars to buy the servers that store this data and the processors that compute it.

This pricing methodology is a root cause of the data architecture problem. The first BI systems to sit on top of these expensive databases assumed database storage would remain expensive forever. But, that key assumption would cease to be true.

Legacy BI: A Three-Layer Cake

The first wave of business intelligence companies started in the early 1990s, building software on the database technologies commercialized by Oracle. Cognos, BusinessObjects, and Microstrategy dominated the era. These companies revolutionized the way their customers accessed data. No longer relying upon a green terminal window and a prompt, users could click their way through an application to create charts and reports.

Seizing the opportunity, Cognos, BusinessObjects, and Microstrategy became monstrously successful businesses. Founded in 1969 and headquartered in Ottawa, Cognos (then named Quasar Corporation) wrote analysis software for mainframes and minicomputers before launching a modern web-based version of its software. In 2011, IBM acquired Cognos for $5 billion on $1.1 billion in revenue. BusinessObjects, a French company, was founded in 1990, and four years later it became the first European software company listed on a U.S. stock exchange. SAP acquired BusinessObjects for more than $7 billion in 2007.

Microstrategy started in 1989, when CEO Michael Saylor sold a $250,000 consulting contract to DuPont. Saylor recruited his friend from MIT, Sanju Basal, to join him. Three years later, the two founders signed McDonald's for a $10 million annual contract, and in 1998 the company went public, doubling its share price on its first day of trading. Today, Microstrategy remains a publicly traded company worth $2 billion.

All three companies built systems that assumed data storage to be expensive. To minimize data storage costs, their engineers would consult with customers in the first week of their contracts. What was the entire list of questions that the business could conceivably ask of its database? With the answer in hand, the BI system would store only the data necessary to answer those precise questions.

Traditional business intelligence systems comprise three layers. An Oracle, or similar, database stores all the company's relevant data. The middle layer, called the data warehouse, siphons data from the database and aggregates figures to create reports. The last layer visualizes the report data and serves it to end users.

Problems with this approach surfaced very quickly. As businesses change, the questions they ask themselves evolve, and in many instances they change dramatically. Each time a business user sought to answer a new question, the data team needed to create a new report within the data warehouse, which took time, effort, and money. As the data warehouse grew, the company paid more to Oracle and other vendors for additional database licenses.

With such a brittle BI architecture, customers couldn't ask and answer new questions. Or they would have to wait weeks, or more, for database teams to adjust the data structure and re-architect the database in order to respond to the organization's new demands. This latency minimized the value that data can have for operations, ultimately dissuading employees from asking pertinent questions and from explaining their actions and making decisions based on real business data.

Within a few years, a few startups would upend this three-layer cake.

Google's Answer to Huge Data: Vanilla Boxes

In the late 1990s, in the Wojcicki garage in Mountain View, California, two Stanford computer science graduate students, Larry Page and Sergey Brin, developed a world-class search engine that used links on web pages as a page-ranking mechanism. But that may have been the easy part.

To answer users' search queries within milliseconds, Page and Brin needed to store previously unheard-of amounts of data. They crawled the burgeoning Internet and stored data about the majority of web pages, even as the number of Internet sites was skyrocketing from hundreds of thousands to millions within just a few years.

Google couldn't afford Oracle's database fees. The data volumes were too massive. So, the Google founders resolved to use inexpensive servers, called vanilla servers because they are plain, inexpensive, and white, that were substantially cheaper than Oracle servers running Oracle's database software.

To manage the titanic volumes of data the Google search crawler would generate as it parsed the Internet, Page and Brin wrote a new proprietary file system called Google File System (GFS) that distributed data across the massive cluster of cheap vanilla servers they had bought.

On top of GFS, Google ran MapReduce, a database engine written by early Google employees Jeffrey Dean and Sanjay Ghemawat, to process the mammoth amounts of data stored in the Google vanilla box cluster. The combination of GFS and MapReduce enabled Google to scale its infrastructure at a tiny fraction of the cost of an Oracle infrastructure. Throughout its more than 16-year history, Google has continued to develop its own databases and file systems to take advantage of low-cost hardware.

As a consequence of such scalable architecture, Google continues to be capable of storing exabytes of data. This data proved to be useful for more than returning answers to the search queries of Google.com visitors. Page and Brin valued empowering employees to use data to understand user needs, and Google provided access to these troves of data from its search index to its advertising products to its application logs, creating the first company with a truly modern data-driven culture.

Since its inception, Google has continued to improve and reinvent the tools that its employees use to analyze data when issues with existing technologies have surfaced. MapReduce is a verbose language, which meant data analysis often took a long time to write and run. In addition, MapReduce provided the same level of data access to everybody. As the company grew, Google added more controls over access to sensitive customer and revenue data.

To address these problems, in 2003, Google engineers Rob Pike, Sean Dorward, Robert Griesemer, and Sean Quinlan wrote Sawzall, the next generation of analytical tools for Google. Compared with MapReduce, Sawzall's language reduced the size of analytical programs by 90 to 95 percent, massively improving data analysis productivity. In addition, Sawzall enabled fine-grained access control, eliding sensitive fields.

Within 18 months of release, Sawzall adoption within Google grew rapidly.

We monitored its use during the month of March 2005. During that time, on one dedicated Workqueue cluster with 1500 Xeon CPUs, there were 32,580 Sawzall jobs launched, using an average of 220 machines each. While running those jobs, 18,636 failures occurred (application failure, network outage, system crash, etc.) that triggered rerunning some portion of the job. The jobs read a total of 3.2×10^{15} bytes of data (2.8PB) and wrote 9.9×10^{12} bytes (9.3TB) (demonstrating that the term "data reduction" has some resonance). The average job therefore processed about 100GB. The jobs collectively consumed almost exactly one machine-century.[3]

At the time, Sawzall code was unique to Google. Its authors provided some basic instructions on syntax, but there was no manual on the open web describing how to write Sawzall code. To train new employees who were unfamiliar with the language, the Sawzall team published all Sawzall code on internal Google websites, available to everyone within the company. This content library enabled people who were curious about data to learn how to write Sawzall code and query the data.

However, the Sawzall language presented some challenges over time. Many people found Sawzall a difficult syntax to learn. In 2006, a Google team led by Shiva Shivakumar developed the next data-processing innovation, Dremel. Unlike Sawzall's unfamiliar dialect, Dremel code was written in structured query language, or SQL, a programming language designed for querying data in relational databases. Developed by IBM researchers Donald Chamberlain and Raymond Boyce in the early 1970s,[4] SQL was first commercialized by Oracle in the early 1980s.

SQL has an elegant and simple syntax. Most SQL queries are of the following form:

SELECT field1, field2, field3 FROM table WHERE condition;

A real query to view the names and total sales of the New York customers of an e-commerce merchant might look like this:

SELECT customer_name, customer_id, total_sales FROM customer_sales_table WHERE customer_state = "New York";

Not all SQL queries are this simple, but they all follow the same structure. And over the past 50 years, SQL has become the de facto

---

[3]Rob Pike, Sean Dorward, Robert Griesemer, and Sean Quinlan, "Interpreting the Data: Parallel Analysis with Sawzall," Google Research Publication, August 13, 2003.
[4]"SQL," Wikipedia. Retrieved March 15, 2016, from https://en.wikipedia.org/wiki/SQL.

or communicating with databases. Even cutting-edge
nvented in the last decade, including Mongo, Cassandra,
NoSQL databases, all speak some form of SQL. Consequently, millions of people around the world know how to write
SQL code. More importantly, as the Dremel team concluded, thousands of SQL-capable employees within Google could analyze data
using Dremel.

Google realized major performance gains over MapReduce with
Dremel, as detailed in the team's 2010 paper. "Some queries achieve
scan throughput close to 100 billion records per second on a shared
cluster," the team reported. The Dremel engineering team conceived
of a new way of storing data in a columnar format that acceler-
ated queries across huge volumes of data. As a consequence, they
observed, "Dremel is able to run aggregation queries over tables with
trillions of rows, and return the results in seconds."[5]

Dremel's impact on Google is impossible to overstate. It has
allowed teams all over the company to deeply understand the trends
within the business and to react to them swiftly.

600 Petabytes per Day: HiPal at Facebook

Like Google, Facebook also aggregates enormous quantities of data.
Every day, Facebook ingests 600 petabytes of data, half of which
is written to disk. To provide some context to the scale, if the 300
petabytes consisted of high-definition movies, a person would need
3,000 years to watch them all. Of those 300 petabytes, Facebook
employees process 10 petabytes per day, mainly to monitor and
understand the results of product experiments on the news feed, on
mobile applications, and elsewhere.[6]

Data analysis is the norm at Facebook. Of the company's 4,600
employees, at least 1,000 query data daily. In total, they execute more
than 10,000 analyses per day, leveraging the infrastructure to help the

---

[5]S. Melnik, A. Gubarev, J. Long, G. Romer, S. Shivakumar, M. Tolton, and T. Vassi-
lakis, "Dremel: Interactive Analysis of Web-Scale Datasets," Google Research Publication, September 13, 2010. Retrieved from http://static.googleusercontent.com/media/
research.google.com/en//pubs/archive/36632.pdf.
[6]"Lifting the Curtain: The Data Infrastructure Behind Facebook Apps," F8 2015, Facebook, March 18, 2015.

company make critical business decisions, drive product changes, and push the groundbreaking company forward.[7]

To provide its employees access to all this data, Facebook has developed a handful of different technologies. All the data is stored in Hadoop, an open-source equivalent of the Google File System. To analyze the data stored in Hadoop, Facebook built a data-warehousing technology named Hive. Like Dremel, Hive receives queries from users in SQL format.

Although many Facebook employees were using Hive to access the data they needed to perform their daily jobs, the majority of the company was unable to write the SQL code necessary to access the data they needed directly. So, the engineering team built a web-based interface to query Hive data and called it HiPal.

HiPal sees heavy use at Facebook from employees who write and execute ad hoc queries. Essentially, HiPal enables users who are not familiar with SQL to perform the same kinds of analyses as those who are SQL-capable. Users can upload their own data sets, combine them with other data, run calculations, and answer their questions quickly. Since the results of their data sets are stored for seven days, employees can share the results with others.

As of 2015, the company records data across 20,000 tables, all accessible to HiPal users. But surfacing the rich data available for analysis became a key challenge for the company. So Facebook developed an internal search tool that helps employees discover the data sets that are available to them and to search within those data sets, including any associated metadata stored by the authors/creators of the data.[8]

This data discovery platform is integrated into HiPal, enabling Facebook employees to find the data they need, and enrich it with other tables and fields, whenever they need it.

---

[7]Anish Thusoo, Zheng Shao, Suresh Anthony, Dhruba Borthakur, Namit Jain, Joydeep Sen Sara, Roghotham Murthy, and Hao Liu, "Data Warehousing and Analytics Infrastructure at Facebook," *Proceedings of the 2010 ACM SIGMOD International Conference on Management of Data*, 1013–1020.

[8]Anish Thusoo, Zheng Shao, Suresh Anthony, Dhruba Borthakur, Namit Jain, Joydeep Sen Sara, Roghotham Murthy, and Hao Liu, "Data Warehousing and Analytics Infrastructure at Facebook," *Proceedings of the 2010 ACM SIGMOD International Conference on Management of Data*, 1013–1020.

This type of data tooling within large Internet companies is not unique to Google and Facebook. LinkedIn has built a very similar data infrastructure, and the data scientists from that team are world-renowned. In fact, D. J. Patil, the former chief data scientist at LinkedIn, became the chief data scientist for the White House.

Extreme Data Collection: The New Normal

Extreme data collection is now the norm. We're finally there. When the first three engineers spin up their first server, they instrument their product. Even the larger companies are doing a better job of shoveling everything into Hadoop. They aren't using it, but it's there waiting to be analyzed.

—Colin Zima

In the past 10 years, companies like Amazon, Google, and Microsoft have built new database products that offer high-performance databases at less than a tenth the cost of traditional databases. Initially, the companies developed these products for internal use. Today, many of the database technologies—Amazon's Redshift and Elastic MapReduce, Google's BigQuery, and Microsoft AzureSQL—are available as a service, enabling customers to store petabytes of data in the cloud, without having to buy their own hardware.

How fast are these databases? FlyData, a Palo Alto–based data-migration company, benchmarked Amazon Redshift's performance. To search through 1.2 terabytes of data, equivalent to the amount of data stored in the 6.1 million books of the Los Angeles Public Library, Redshift took no more than 10 seconds.[9]

This seismic shift in the database ecosystem invalidates the key assumption of the very first business intelligence companies: that not all of a company's relevant data could be stored cost-effectively in

---

[9]FlyData Team, "With Amazon Redshift SSD, Querying a TB of Data Took Less than 10 Seconds," FlyData, January 29, 2014. Retrieved from https://www.flydata.com/blog/with-amazon-redshift-ssd-querying-a-tb-of-data-took-less-than-10-seconds/.

a single database. Instead, these massive database systems can run queries across billions of records in fractions of seconds. So why subset the data in a data warehouse?

Offering massive data addressability, huge cost reductions, and deep granularity, today's modern databases demand a parallel retooling of the analytics that access them. Otherwise, all the data we're collecting in these databases is useless, like molding books rotting in a forgotten corner of the library.

Google's Sawzall and Dremel and Facebook's HiPal prove the point that legacy business analytics software doesn't meet the needs of a new generation of data scientists and analysts. Nor do legacy products leverage the monumental performance advances of the past decade to enable new types of analysis and new types of businesses.

Now that companies routinely collect extreme amounts of data, we have the opportunity to extract insight from those petabytes.

Looker: Weaving the Data Fabric

As employees from web-scale Internet companies like Google, Facebook, and LinkedIn leave to found new businesses or become key contributors at existing businesses, they carry with them an expectation that the same types of data discovery tools will exist in their new jobs. Whether they're data scientists or mainstream businesspeople, they have granular questions and they demand a responsive data environment to support their work.

Looker was founded to satisfy the needs of this new cadre of data-savvy experts. As the Internet continues to drive change at every level across functions and industries, innovation among early business intelligence pioneers has failed to keep up. Where are the tools that make sense for a new way of doing business?

THE BIRTH OF BIG DATA

How did we arrive at this new world of data-driven businesses? We can probably credit Big Data. Big Data gave us cheap, fast, infinitely scalable systems. Originally, Big Data was the result of the counterterrorism movement after 9/11, when security fears dictated the collection of vast amounts of machine-generated data. This was also around the time of Web 2.0, when a surge of user-generated content and Internet interactivity resulted in gigantic stores of user and event data, before anyone had a clue what to do with it.

The brightest teams in computer science responded to the Big Data phenomenon with a revolution in data management infrastructure, primarily around scale-out massively parallel processing databases, MapReduce and Hadoop. Many new tools, like Palantir, focused on the hard work of data science, largely around predictive analytics. Companies like Splunk focused on computer log data. Yet other businesses like Tableau focused on departmental solutions, creating the conflicts we now know to be associated with data silos. There were some advances among analytic tools, but no great revolution.

Even as Hadoop gathered momentum, a new generation of analytic databases saw the light of day. From Greenplum to Vertica, HANA to Redshift, processing capabilities around large data sets were growing at incredible speed. These systems used fresh techniques, such as column-oriented data storage, in-memory processing, and MPP scale-out, to bring new power to the analytic ecosystem and to business decision making.

Finally, there was an affordable way to store huge data sets, but unfortunately, the only workable interface was hand-coded SQL or MapReduce. Specialized data scientists and analysts had their work cut out for them, as decision makers in marketing, finance, and operations piled on the questions. Data breadlines ensued.

A DATA-HUNGRY WORKFORCE, FED BY LOOKER

A Data Hungry Workforce

—Frank Bien

The world has changed in another important way. The people who are graduating from school now grew up with the Internet. They are digital natives. If they have a question, they want to look up the answer, then and there.

Data is cool. It's not the old world where everyone is operating in PowerPoint. Instead they're operating in spreadsheets, charts, graphs, and hard numbers—and Nate Silver is their hero.

This young workforce also interacts with software differently. They don't care as much about interface and ease of use, the stuff we used to think was important. What they want is code. Data economists, not even the super-hardcore techy people, are more comfortable operating in a bit of code, exposing the process, and knowing how they got the result they're looking at.

BEYOND BI—AN ENTIRELY NEW KIND OF DATA TOOL

So there we were: Gigantic data sets, really flexible database architectures, super-smart data scientists and programmers, and a data-hungry workforce—but we didn't have a way to bring them together.

Even by 2012, the core of BI technology was stuck in 2002. We never had BI 2.0. Instead, we had a "dumbing down" of BI. Dashboards replaced data scientists. Analytics needed to be brain-dead easy to use, with slick user interfaces for reducing complex data into pretty graphics.

But how can you see into the data—all the data—and find value in it? Now that you can store everything, how can you interact with it? How come you can't click around, and one thing leads to the next, leads to the next, leads to the next? That's what happened when people first started using Google. Why can't you have this completely new experience of your company's data?

When Looker entered the business world, in 2012, our vision was to deliver HTML for data. Looker was conceived through a love affair between data and languages. It grew up out of the web, the world of Google and Facebook, Ruby and JavaScript, Slack and Github, and the emerging class of modern data analysts and scientists. It grew out of database and language experts, not the enterprise software BI crowd. And it grew up in a hybrid world of MySQL, MPP, columnar, and Hadoop/Hive data management infrastructures.

LOOKER—A NEW WAY TO DO DATA

How did Looker put this HTML-like vision into action? Our product, also called Looker, works by getting a customized data query interface into the hands of business users so they can ask and answer very complex business data questions, getting down to the row level on any inquiry. Of course, in order to deliver that kind of capability, there's customization. And in Looker, that customization is performed in a language called LookML, a language we invented.

Using LookML, data analysts develop a model that defines the relationships in the database and the metrics that are important to the business, creating a single source of truth for the entire organization. The result is a customized, web-based application that allows anyone in the company to download, explore, save, and share data, without needing to know SQL. As it turns out, this quick-to-learn environment fuels curiosity, rather than simply returning pixel-perfect reports and dashboards on a periodic basis.

So where are we now? Looker operates within the new era of scalable databases, and our LookML models can see everything in them. Our agile data-modeling language enables a new kind of usability. It's not about dumbing down BI "so the CEO can use it." Instead, it's about creating such compelling value that *any* user can, and will, become immersed directly in the data, including the CEO. The new world is an interconnected web of things, boatloads of content, married with exploration and the freedom to trip over the things you didn't even know you needed. This is the modern data fabric.

Chapter 4

Achieving Data Enlightenment: Gathering Data in the Morning and Changing Your Business's Operations in the Afternoon

Not Just Another Person with an Opinion

Without data you're just another person with an opinion.
—W. Edwards Deming

In 2013, *The Economist* studied the data strategies of 530 companies.[1] Those executives who considered their companies to be ahead of their peers in the use of data cited culture as the single biggest contributor to becoming a data-driven company. Unifying the silos, digitizing the card catalog, quelling the brawls, and satisfying the breadlines are all necessary steps, but inculcating a data-driven culture is far more fundamental.

What do we mean by data-driven? Most every company in the world today depends on data. But the vast majority of them use data in retrospect, to understand history, not to drive decisions.

Does the prevalent use of dashboards mean a company is data-driven? A collection of metrics smattered on a wall-mounted television screen or e-mailed twice a day certainly can inform

---

[1] *The Economist* Intelligence Unit, "Decisive Action: How Businesses Make Decisions and How They Could Do It Better," n.d. Retrieved January 29, 2016, from www.economistinsights.com/sites/default/files/Decisive Action - How businesses make decisions.pdf.

management about its company's progress, but we believe it's not enough. Dashboards don't usually change the way employees operate the business.

When we say data-driven, we're talking about companies that operationalize data. We're talking about businesspeople who use data to change the way they work right now and later this afternoon, who consult data before developing new products, speaking to customers, or designing an ad campaign. We were talking about workers who wake up every morning and use data to tune their actions throughout the day.

In a recent report, Forrester Research stated: "We have entered a new age—one in which the attitudes, rules, and behaviors that govern how firms use data are radically transforming. Highly agile startups and flat organizations are giving vast numbers of employees direct access to customer data and the tools they need to explore it, test out hypotheses, and inform the decisions they make daily."[2]

Several companies are innovating in a 600-year-old industry: secondhand clothing. Both The RealReal and ThredUp use data to manage their businesses, develop competitive advantages, and sustain their tremendous growth.

SECONDHAND CLOTHING—A NEW RENAISSANCE

From 1500 to 1650, Venice experienced its golden age. The city's printers were the finest in the world and its schools educated some of greatest architects, including the notable architect Palladio. Venetian patrons invested in an exquisite painting school that produced Titian. His paintings are still considered rivals of works by Leonardo, Michelangelo, and Raphael, of Florence and Rome.

Tailors in the city plied the finest fabrics to satisfy the desires of their wealthy patrons. In Italy's sixteenth century, many artisans, including tailors, belonged to guilds, called *scuoli*, that existed to support schools in their particular trades. Each guild was authorized by the government and given one of two statuses, either *piccolo* (lesser) or *grande* (greater). These guilds served several functions,

---

[2]T. Costa, J. Dalton, A. Burnette, and C. Stearns, "The Data-Driven Design Revolution," August 5, 2014. Retrieved from https://www.forrester.com/The DataDriven Design Revolution/fulltext/-/E-res115903.

including apprenticing new artisans across many different disciplines. The tailors' guild was granted the *grande* status, and membership carried with it considerable nobility, in part because of the cost of fabric.

"[The] merchants knew that even used garments, if made of silk, were not beneath the dignity of a Venetian nobleman. Indeed, it was common for patricians to borrow secondhand silk clothes and other objects from strazzaroli (secondhand dealers)."[3]

The strazzaroli guild continued to flourish within Italy and throughout France and Britain for several hundred years until the spinning jenny, the water frame, and the power loom industrialized clothing manufacture.

Eventually, machines replaced sartorialists, and clothiers could produce attire by the truckload. Millions of people could afford new clothes for the first time. As clothing production surged, the secondhand clothing market collapsed.

Today, ThredUp and The RealReal are reinvigorating that market.

COLLABORATION AROUND RAPID PRODUCT CONVERSION—THE REALREAL

Founded in 2011 by Julie Wainwright, The RealReal is a 300-person luxury consignment company with projected revenue of more than $200 million in 2015.[4] Based in Tiburon, California, a wealthy San Francisco suburb nestled on the north side of San Francisco Bay, the company offers the Internet's largest selection of preowned and authenticated luxury items, for both men and women. When someone consigns high-end clothing, jewelry, watches, art, or other luxury products, a member of The RealReal's concierge team visits the owner's home, chooses the items that meet the company's high standards, authenticates them, and takes the merchandise away to be sold on the website.

---

[3]L. Molà, *The Silk Industry of Renaissance Venice* (Baltimore: Johns Hopkins University Press, 2000).

[4]S. Perez, "Luxury Consignment Site The RealReal Adds $40 Million in New Funding," *TechCrunch*, April 9, 2015. Retrieved from http://techcrunch.com/2015/04/09/luxury-consignment-site-the-realreal-adds-40-million-in-new-funding/http://techcrunch.com/2015/04/09/luxury-consignment-site-the-realreal-adds-40-million-in-new-funding/.

To succeed, The RealReal must sell consigned inventory quickly. Unlike traditional high-end consignment boutiques, The RealReal employs data to manage its business.

Every morning, Chris Deyo, EVP of operations at The RealReal, looks at a real-time report to gauge the status of both warehouses and every product in the internal value chain. Each inbound product must be tagged with an SKU number, photographed, uploaded, stocked on shelves, and made ready to be shipped as soon as a customer buys it.

At a moment's glance, Chris can understand exactly how the warehouses are performing today relative to previous days. He can also see the size of the inbound queue and how long it will take to be tagged and stocked. Last, he can understand where the delays in the entire process might be, so he can correct problems before they bog down the business.

Chris isn't the only data-savvy manager at The RealReal. At 4 p.m. each day, the entire executive team uses data to understand daily revenues. If the company is behind, an alert is sent to the marketing and merchandising teams, who dynamically create an end-of-day content marketing plan that might include an e-mail blast to a particular customer segment or an in-app mobile message promoting a particular type of product. This immediate response in the afternoon ensures the company consistently achieves its daily revenue targets, and consequently its annual goals.

Because everyone in the company is looking at exactly the same data set, everyone is always on the same page about how the company ought to react to the data. The marketing, merchandising, finance, and executive teams can collaborate effectively and immediately to meet shifting demands throughout the day.

This is what we mean by operationalizing data: changing the way a company operates in the afternoon based on the data from the morning.

OPERATIONAL COMPLEXITY AT SCALE—THREDUP

Founded in 2009 by three friends—James Reinhardt, Chris Homer, and Oliver Lubin—living in Cambridge, Massachusetts, ThredUp initially experimented with swapping secondhand men's shirts. A year later, when they refocused the business on women and children's clothing, demand skyrocketed, fueling the company's rapid growth. In 2015, *Forbes* named ThredUp one of America's Most Promising Companies and the leader in gently worn clothes.[5]

How does ThredUp work? First, a user signs up and requests an empty ThredUp bag. A few days later, a green polka-dot polyester bag arrives by mail. Families fill the bags with their gently worn children's and women's clothing and send them back to ThredUp for sale on the ThredUp site, receiving a share of the value.

The company now employs almost 500 people in five or six different locations across the United States, many of whom work to evaluate, photograph, and catalog incoming items and to pick, pack, and ship outgoing items.

The operational complexity in a ThredUp distribution center is massive. Every day, the company processes tens of thousands of new clothing items that arrive by the truckload. For each item, a ThredUp employee catalogs tens of attributes, such as the brand, the size, the style, the color, and the condition of the garment.

All of these data points feed an algorithm that calculates the expected value of the item, which includes a prediction of the selling price and the time to sell the item. These predictions enable the company to select which items to keep and which items to sell on the secondary clothing market at bulk rates. This process is repeated for tens of thousands of items per day across hundreds of employees.

ThredUp's operational success is fueled by data. With literally tons of clothes coming and going every day, the company must track the location of each item, understand its characteristics, merchandise it well, and minimize the processing time from inbound evaluation to outbound shipping. To handle such complexity at scale, the company hired the data team that built the DVD operations at Netflix.

Relentless focus on improving performance has enabled ThredUp to scale quickly, increase profit margins many fold, and replicate a robust processing model across distribution centers. Monitors dot the walls of the ThredUp facilities, showing employee leaderboards and key performance indicators.

---

[5] "America's Most Promising Companies," *Forbes*, January 2015. Retrieved from www .forbes.com/companies/thredup/.

For example, each warehouse employee inputs processing data and keeps an eye on his own performance. How many items is he identifying? How many of these identifications are correct? How does this efficiency compare with that of his peers? It all rolls into labor and processing cost that is managed on a daily basis for inbound clothing, items that come into the ThredUp distribution center, and for outbound clothing, items that customers have purchased.

In addition, this information is presented to the operations team in real time, displayed on monitors across the distribution centers, and reported to management to ensure the company, and every employee, is achieving its target efficiencies.

FINDING CUSTOMER LOVE—THREDUP

The distribution center data also informs the strategies of ThredUp's marketers and merchandisers. Customer information, such as who is purchasing, who isn't, and how those trends change with time, is a critical component of ThredUp's marketing strategy. Customer loyalty varies by demographics, geographic location of customers, seasons, and whether or not customers are new or repeat buyers.

How can you tell if you have a loyal customer? Al Ghorai, senior vice president of finance, planning, and analytics at ThredUp, described three critical loyalty signals that help the company's marketing team understand how to better serve ThredUp's customer base.[6]

1. How engaged are your customers? "We look at what users buy. Do they buy all women's? All kid's? Do they buy a mix? For us, if you're buying a mix of clothes … a customer is at a higher level of engagement." An engaged buyer may not require a discount to incent them to continue buying.
2. What devices did they use to buy? "Did they buy on the web, in the native application [on iOS], or on mobile web? … If you start on web, and then buy on Android or iOS, then you have integrated us into your life." The value of

---

the cross-channel interaction suggests that ThredUp should entice new customers to use the product on another platform or device.

3. What channel was used to acquire new customers? Did they arrive at ThredUp organically (from a search) or via a paid acquisition channel, such as an application download, an affiliate link, or a referral? "If we paid to acquire you, do we have to pay again to drive a second order, or have we done a good enough job to bring you back naturally/organically?" Understanding the customer journey from first acquisition to subsequent orders can help save on marketing costs.

Two key assets underpin the operations at ThredUp and The Real-Real. First, flexible, modern data infrastructures enable these businesses to react as quickly as the fashion industry changes. Prices for clothing fluctuate with supply and demand. Key metrics are shared across the company to ensure the business keeps pace with hourly projects to ultimately attain its daily goals.

Second, both of these businesses inculcate data-driven cultures. Culture is the way within a company that people communicate and collaborate to solve problems. It's amorphous and hard to define, but when you work in a company with a great culture, the result is plain to see. ThredUp and The RealReal approach their market in ways that will provide them a long-term competitive advantage in each of their segments.

THE BIKE RACK EFFECT: COMBATING FRIVOLITY IN MEETINGS

Just as you would not permit a fellow employee to steal a piece of office equipment, you shouldn't let anyone walk away with the time of his fellow managers.

—Andy Grove

Imagine a company meeting with three agenda items: a $100 million data center approval, a request to build a $10,000 bike rack for employees, and a $100 proposal to buy organic lemonade for the annual picnic. The data center discussion takes all of three minutes to reach approval, as does the refreshment budget. But the $10,000 bike rack debate drags on for hours as executive team members debate the right materials, the best color scheme, and the right way to announce the project. This is the bike rack effect.

We've all been in meetings like this. Also known as Parkinson's Law of Triviality, the bike rack effect reflects the reality that companies spend a disproportionate amount of time on trivial issues.

How time consuming can meetings be? Bain Capital partnered with VoloMetrix to quantify the time consumed by meetings across 17 large corporations. At one company, they tallied the impact of a weekly three-hour executive team meeting over the course of a year.[7]

The executives who attended this meeting spent 7,000 hours each year in the meetings themselves. The 11 business unit heads who needed to prepare materials for these meetings spent another 20,000 hours with their teams, who consequently scheduled meetings with 21 other reports deeper in the organization, adding 63,000 hours to the annual tally. To prepare and review the material, this legion of teams invested another 210,000 hours in 130 preparatory meetings.

The annual total to support one weekly executive meeting: 300,000 hours, or about 150 person-years. How many bike racks can a team debate in that amount of time?

There is another way. Incisive data combats this vortex. It slashes debate time in meetings by focusing an executive team, or any functional team, on the right questions.

Data Proves the Point—Metrics-Based Decisions at Zendesk

At Zendesk, a publicly traded maker of customer support software, the product team and marketing teams held a meeting to discuss the release of a new advanced reporting feature. Zendesk's standard reporting tools enabled its customers to view their teams' metrics, such as the median time-to-resolution for customer e-mails and response time by customer service rep. With the new advanced analytics, customer service managers could analyze the data in a myriad of new ways.

The two teams aimed to answer this question: Should we use a marketing campaign to inform those customers who had requested

---

[7]M. Mankins, C. Brahm, and G. Caimi, "Your Scarcest Resource," *Harvard Business Review*, May 2014. Retrieved from https://hbr.org/2014/05/your-scarcest-resource.

advanced analytics in the past? The product team, motivated to onboard as many users employing the new features as possible, pushed for a marketing campaign.

The marketing team, on the other hand, wondered whether the effort was worth the time investment. In particular, Katherine, a young product marketing manager, wondered whether the size of the potential customer base merited the effort to design, distribute, and measure this campaign. As the debate bounced back and forth on whether to launch the campaign, Katherine sat quietly for a few minutes, digging through the company's data on her laptop.

Katherine interrupted the meeting: "There are 27 customers in the segment we're talking about." The meeting room fell silent. Twenty-seven customers represented less than 0.03 percent of Zendesk's customer base. The answer was clear: no marketing campaign. Like the lemonade, the issue wasn't worth spending any time on, and with just a bit of data, the answer became obvious to everyone. That 10-minute investment to research the question saved the 10 people in the room 30 minutes, or collectively more than five hours of discussion.

This Zendesk meeting highlights an important but underappreciated facet of data analysis: The results don't always need to be incredibly accurate. Oftentimes, directional data provides just as much value as very high resolution data. Had Katherine's figure been 2, 27, or 270, the answer would have remained the same, despite a 100× difference in the aggregate amount. Compared with the total size of the Zendesk customer base, such small customer segments wouldn't have warranted a significant outreach campaign.

As a result of case studies like this one, the Zendesk team trains their employees on ballparking, the skill to estimate the order of magnitude of a result before investing a substantial amount of time to calculate the precise answer. Many times, a quick approximation provides just the guidance the team needs to decide the relative priority of an effort or new project.

And the data proves the point. According to a report conducted by the SAS Institute, "More than 70 percent of the organizations that had deployed analytics throughout their organizations reported improved financial performance, increased productivity, reduced risks, and faster decision-making. Organizations with less widespread distribution of analytics access were typically 20 percentage points less likely to report such benefits."[8]

It's pure magic when these conversations are informed by data. That's the vision of data-driven embodied businesses. Teams become more effective. They consistently make better decisions. They focus on the areas of greatest leverage for themselves and their businesses. And years of precious time are salvaged from bike rack meetings and returned to the productivity pool.

DISRUPTING WITH DATA: FOUR CASE STUDIES

You are not entitled to your opinion. You are entitled to your informed opinion. No one is entitled to be ignorant.

—Harlan Ellison

DISRUPTING A MILAN MONOPOLIST

Warby Parker is a rebellious company. Founded in Philadelphia in 2009 by Dave Gilboa and his classmates at the Wharton School of the University of Pennsylvania, Warby Parker challenges a $30 billion Italian hegemon, Luxottica. With an estimated 60 percent market share of U.S. eyeglasses and sunglasses, Luxottica dominates the eyewear industry.[9]

Luxottica taxes the typical American at every step of the buying journey for eyeglasses. Each month, 39 million Americans pay monthly fees for eye care insurance to EyeMed, the second largest eye-care insurer in the United States. It's owned by Luxottica.[10] Those Americans might visit the optometrist once per year. The eye

---

[8]"The Evolution of Decision Making: How Leading Organizations Are Adopting a Data-Driven Culture," *Harvard Business Review*, 2012. Retrieved from https://hbr .org/resources/pdfs/tools/17568_HBR_SAS Report_webview.pdf.

[9]"Is Competition In the Eyewear Segment Preying over Luxottica's Bottom Line?," GuruFocus, February 24, 2015. Retrieved from www.gurufocus.com/news/ 318329/is-competition-in-the-eyewear-segment-preying-over-luxotticas-bottom-linehttp://www.gurufocus.com/news/318329/is-competition-in-the-eyewear-segment-preying-over-luxotticas-bottom-line.

[10.] "EyeMed Vision Care," Luxottica, n.d. Retrieved from www.luxottica.com/en/our-way/our-business-model/eyemed-vision-care.

doctor is quite likely employed by Luxottica. Despite the diversity in the brands adorning the frames stored in glass cabinets around the store, all of the glasses are Luxottica. In fact, Sunglass Hut, LensCrafters, Sears Optical, Pearle Vision, and Target Optical all belong to Luxottica. And the lenses within those new frames? They will be sent to a Luxottica-owned lens maker, accreting more revenues to the Milan-based monopolist.

To compete with Luxottica's vertical integration, Warby Parker pursued a radically different approach in three ways. First, Warby Parker is mission-driven, and its corporate status reflects it. While most enterprises in the United States are C corporations, Warby Parker is a B corp. B corps are pro-profit companies that are explicitly mission-driven. In addition to maximizing shareholder value, the goal of nearly all corporations, benefit corporations strive to impact society and the environment in a positive way. The charter of a B corp dictates that the board of directors must consider the best interests of the corporation and the effects of its decisions on the company's workforce, its customers, community and societal factors, and the environment. Quite a difference from Luxottica.

Second, Warby Parker initially sold to customers exclusively online. Eschewing retail locations, the company invented the Home Try-On program. Customers browse frames in Warby Parker's collection on their laptop or mobile phone, choose five they like, and receive them a few days later by mail. At home.

Third, Warby Parker uses data extensively. Carl Andersen is the director of data science at Warby Parker. A PhD in mathematical biology from the University of Sheffield, Carl oversees many of the different programs intended to convert data into competitive advantages for Warby Parker.

The data from the Home Try-On program informs Warby Parker's merchandise. Models that are requested for Home Try-On but are never purchased are scrapped. The data team notes characteristics of the more successful models and relays that information to designers and merchandisers. This kind of data-driven optimization has powered the company's growth to more than $100 million.

To supplement the Internet-based Home Try-On program, Warby Parker has opened 13 dedicated stores and 13 showrooms within other stores across the United States. Customer satisfaction within the stores is a key priority for the company, so the Warby Parker data team sends surveys to the people who visit their stores.

All of the survey data is aggregated in a centralized database. Each morning, store managers receive an automatically generated e-mail containing the most important customer feedback about their store. During the winter of 2014, one dissatisfied customer wrote that the Manhattan flagship store wasn't a great experience because of the germs. At the height of the New York cold season, customers model frames in between sneezes and coughs. Who wants to try on potentially infectious frames? So the customer requested hand sanitizer throughout the store.

The morning after this customer's visit, the head of the Manhattan store received the feedback e-mail, stopped at a local pharmacy on the way to work, and placed hand sanitizer at key places inside the store. Customer satisfaction for that store returned to its normally high levels.

This is a great example of operationalizing data: The manager receives feedback in the morning about how to improve operations for the store and rectifies the problem before noon. It's not just the CEO, the analyst team, or the finance team that uses data in a truly data-driven company. It's everyone.

Aligning Sales Teams in Real Time

HubSpot is a $1.5 billion iconoclast of a company. Founded in 2006 at MIT by Brian Halligan and Dharmesh Shah, HubSpot created the inbound marketing wave, and its orange logo is synonymous with efficient content marketing and customer acquisition, particularly for small-to-medium businesses. Since its founding, HubSpot has become the third most popular marketing automation software by market share.

In 2015, the company generated more than $150 million in revenue. To sustain the business's 50 percent annual revenue growth rate, the sales team employs a quantitative promotion plan for its salespeople, removing any element of personal judgment. HubSpot salespeople are measured on five metrics, in addition to bookings.

Pipeline size: HubSpot measures pipeline size by the number of contacts a customer manages. Today, pricing varies between

$200 per month to $2,400 per month, depending on the size of the customer's customer database.

Deal velocity: Each salesperson is assigned a quota that varies with his region, his experience, and his industry. The combination of these three factors influences the average value of a customer a salesperson pursues. Deal velocity divides the total quota by the average value of a customer, allowing the salesperson to determine the number of customers he must close each week in order to attain his quota.

Cash collection characteristics: Many customers buy a 12-month subscription for HubSpot software. Some customers are willing to pay for all 12 months at sign-up. The more a customer is willing to pay at the beginning of the contract, the more cash HubSpot has to fuel its growth over the subsequent 12 months, so salespeople are incentivized to structure contracts with annual prepay.

Quota attainment rate: The quota attainment rate is the ratio of currently retired quota to target quota. Retired quota is the total value of all new contracts in the current quarter.

Customer retention: Inevitably, some HubSpot customers who have signed a contract will decide not to renew their contract in one year. In contrast, other customers, the valuable ones, increase their spend over time as they add more and more contacts to their HubSpot database. Customer retention measures the value of a cohort of customers over time. If the salesperson is selecting his target customers well, the customers he closed last year should be paying more in aggregate this year, implying that they are happy with the software and are succeeding with it. The contrary may also be true: If the salesperson is selling to customers for whom the product is not a good fit, many of them will no longer renew the software or will pay less for it in the future.

Obviously, this cocktail of metrics isn't a simple formula for salespeople to understand and calculate themselves. So, the sales operations team has built an embedded dashboard within Salesforce that displays these crucial metrics. Salespeople can access their dashboard whenever they like to see precisely where they are at any point in time during the quarter relative to their goal.

HubSpot has found that this consistent feedback and quantitative measurement enable sales leaders to coach the sales team to close exactly the customers who will ultimately be successful with HubSpot's software and will continue to drive its sensational growth.

Scaling Sales Teams with Data

At the same time, the data used to inform salespeople of their metrics can also be reframed to empower sales managers to lead a high-performance sales organization. For example, as new salespeople join the team, how fast are they ramping? How quickly does a new account executive begin to close customers and attain his full quota?

As new salespeople join a business, they are provided a ramp time, a period to learn the sales processes, learn the product, study the typical objections, and develop their own techniques to succeed. At the beginning of the ramp, the salespeople are responsible for 25 percent of their full quota. As they learn the company's product and sales motions, this quota responsibility ramps to 100 percent. Ramp times vary depending on the value of the product and the length of the sales cycle.

Salespeople typically come in one of two varieties. Inside sales representatives close customers primarily through the telephone. They work inside the business. Typically, inside salespeople ramp within one to three quarters.

Outside salespeople, or field salespeople, travel quite a bit and spend the bulk of their time outside their office. In the software world, inside sales quotas vary from $400,000 to $1.2 million. Outside sales representatives tend to carry quotas of $1 million to $2.5 million, though sometimes they can close substantially more business. Larger contracts often imply elongated sales cycles spanning 6 to 12 months. To evaluate the performance of field salespeople, sales managers often require more time, so field ramp times range from 6 to 12 months.

As salespeople enter and exit the organization, a sales manager must manage each individual's performance to maximize the success of the organization. At any given time, some salespeople might be ramping, others may have just been promoted and assigned a higher quota, and still others may have moved from inside to field. The amount of business a sales team books relative to their goal, quota targets and quota retirement, will often change daily.

At Looker, sales managers use the report shown in Figure 4.1 to measure the performance of their inside sales and field sales teams. In the first column, the report lists each salesperson. (An *I* indicates an inside salesperson and an *O* indicates an outside rep.) Calendar quarters are demarcated across the top.

In Looker's case, the ramp period for both inside and outside salespeople extends six months, or two quarters. For each rep, the first box, which spans that two-quarter ramp period, indicates when the rep started. During this six-month ramp time, the reps have a smaller target quota and the rep's performance relative to that target is contained within the box. A 100 percent means the salesperson booked exactly his quota. Less than 100 percent implies he missed his number; greater than 100 percent means he exceeded his target quota.

This visualization shows exactly how sales reps are progressing through their ramps and how they matured within the organization.

Rep	Q3 2013	Q4 2013	Q1 2014	Q2 2014	Q3 2014	Q4 2014		Pipeline/ Quota
Cailin Cloutier (I)	156%		65%	37%	47%	143%		1.2
Holden Johnson (I)		1%		64%	10%	140%		3.5
Laurence Woodward (O)		73%		138%	145%	24%		2.4
Roberta Collins (O)			140%		137%	145%		1.6
Sarah Read (I)			32%		120%	90%		1.0
Steve Tennison (O)					7%			2.0
Gemma Anabel (I)					14%			3.7

FIGURE 4.1   Looker's Sales Productivity Report

Each subsequent box in a rep's role indicates how the rep's quota attainment progresses with time and whether or not the rep is consistently attaining quota.

The last column on the right indicates the pipeline-to-quota ratio, which divides the total value of the rep's qualified pipeline by the target quota for the period. This is a leading indicator of whether the salesperson will be able to attain his quota in the current period.

Ideally, the booking-to-quota ratio should be between four and five. If a company's lead-to-close rate is 20 percent—in other words, if one in five leads converts to a customer—the pipeline-to-quota ratio should be at least five, or 1/20. If the close rate is 25 percent, the target pipeline-to-quota ratio should be four. The better the close rate, the smaller the ratio needs to be in order for reps to consistently attain quota.

Determining Customer Satisfaction at Every Point in the Buyer Journey

He called his first startup Caput, meaning "the head" in Latin. Caput built online communities for large European companies around the turn of the millennium. Caput sold software through others, called value-added resellers (VARs), that would customize the base software to the needs of very large enterprises. In the dot-com crash of the early 2000s, VARs struggled to stay afloat. Caput went kaput. The irony didn't escape Mikkel Svane, the CEO and Danish computer scientist.

He and his cofounders Morten Primdahl and Alexander Aghassipour shut down Kaput and went to work for Materna, a large Scandinavian consultancy for a few years, when inspiration struck them again as they sat in Svane's living room.

> "If we don't do this now, we will end up as 'butt cheek consultants,'" said Morten. He's probably the only person in the world to use that term—an allusion to the common scalloped curtains called 'butt-cheek curtains' that hung in ordinary Danish homes.[11]

[11]Mikkel Svane and Carlye Adler, *Startupland: How Three Guys Risked Everything to Turn an Idea into a Global Business* (San Francisco: Jossey-Bass, 2015), 18.

At Materna, Svane and his teammates sold sophisticated, heavy and complex customer support software to multinationals. After deployment, the team "saw organ rejection and had to cut back on advanced functionality, one limb at a time." Management was deploying these solutions to contain costs within the customer service center. And no one buying the software cared about the experience for the customer representative. Was the software intuitive? Did it enhance productivity? Were agents happier?

The triumvirate saw the opportunity to build the software that would be bought by the customer service representatives themselves, because it was built explicitly for them—a drastic departure from the competitive monolithic software sold to top-down executives.

So, in 2007, Svane, Primdahl, and Aghassipour resolved to build the business they envisioned. They called it Zendesk for the peace and calm they would instill in their users.

Worth more than $2 billion, Zendesk serves more than 100,000 businesses today, providing the software that helps customer service representatives answer customer inquiries by e-mail, chat, and telephone.

Zendesk grew to more than $70 million in revenue just six years after Mikkel cofounded it. Amazingly, the company achieved this by aggregating tens of thousands of small customers, each paying about $2,000 per year. In 2015, the company recorded more than $200 million in annual revenue.

As Mikkel relates in his book *Startupland*, the company relentlessly pursued simplicity in their product. A sharp contrast to the complex, unwieldy software they replaced, a Zendesk customer service center could be set up in minutes, not weeks. The product was received by customer support leaders as a revelation, and the company enjoyed a hugely positive reception in the community. Quickly, this enthusiasm spread by word of mouth and the company began its sensational growth.

How did the Zendesk team quantify this exuberance? They used a metric called Net Promoter Score. Bain & Co. developed the Net Promoter Score, or NPS, in the early 2000s to measure customer loyalty. It is measured on a scale from +100 to –100 and is gathered by sending out a survey to customers asking each one, "How likely are you to recommend this product to a friend or colleague?" The recipient answers on a scale from 1 to 10.

Respondents who mark 9 or 10 on the survey are Promoters. Those who mark 0 to 6 are Detractors. The remainder are dubbed Passives. The NPS is calculated by subtracting the number of Promoters from Detractors. At the bottom of the heap, companies like Time Warner Cable register −20 NPS.[12] In 2015, Costco recorded the highest NPS of all Fortune 500 companies, at 79.[13]

The typical software company receives an NPS of 29, meaning there are only slightly more Promoters than Detractors.[14] But at its peak, Zendesk charted an NPS of 90! For every one detractor of Zendesk, there were nine other people recommending it to friends and colleagues.

Best-in-class NPS scores meaningfully reduce the cost to acquire customers, greasing the marketing engine and powering revenue growth. This hugely positive force has propelled the company's growth and enabled it to scale across borders quickly. Before Zendesk had an office or a single employee in Brazil, it counted a thousand customers, all from word of mouth. And the customer base was growing at 300 percent annually.[15]

Unlike many companies who use NPS to survey existing customers, Zendesk polls its users at three different points during the sales cycle: (1) immediately after signing up; (2) a few days after signing up as a customer, potentially having spoken to salesperson,

[12]B. Rocks, "2015 Consumer NPS Benchmarks Study—Part III: Entertainment & Telecom," *Satmetrix*, July 7, 2015. Retrieved from http://blog.satmetrix.com/2015-consumer-nps-benchmarks-study-part-iii-entertainment-telecom.

[13]"Costco, USAA, Amazon.com and Apple Rank Among Highest In Customer Loyalty in Latest Satmetrix Net Promoter Benchmarks," *Satmetrix*, March 31, 2016. Retrieved from www.satmetrix.com/in-the-news/costco-usaa-amazon-and-apple-rank-among-highest-in-customer-loyalty-in-latest-satmetrix-net-promoter-benchmarks/.

[14]"The Zendesk Benchmark," Zendesk, January 2015. Retrieved from https://d26a57ydsghvgx.cloudfront.net/content/resources/zendesk-benchmark-Q1-2015.pdf

[15]"Zendesk Launches in Brazil with 1,000 Customers," Zendesk, August 27, 2013. Retrieved from https://www.zendesk.com/company/press/zendesk-launches-brazil-1000-customers-br/.

and beginning to pay for the service; and (3) some time after the customer has been using the product.

Structuring the NPS survey this way helps the Zendesk team isolate which teams influence the NPS and which actions correspond to positive and negative fluctuations. The first test chronologically establishes the positive impact of the marketing team on customers' and prospects' perceptions of Zendesk. The second survey establishes the happiness of the customer immediately after purchasing the product, and the product team's effectiveness in developing the right on-boarding experience. The third NPS measures ongoing satisfaction and whether the product has met the customer's expectations over time, again measuring marketing and sales.

If NPS spikes right after the sale and falls during the third survey, this is a sign the customer has been oversold—the company has overpromised the customer and these expectations haven't been fulfilled, which could rapidly weaken the word-of-mouth growth of the product. Structuring NPS surveys this way enables Zendesk to measure customer satisfaction through the buyer journey and isolate the effects of different teams.

Summary

Warby Parker, Hubspot, Looker, and Zendesk each use data in different ways to gain a competitive edge. Whether it's merchandising inventory better, measuring and responding to customer requests faster, ramping salespeople sooner, or incenting go-to-market teams properly, data underpins all these processes.

The Rosetta Stone: Developing a Shared Data Language

How do teams operationalize data in the same way that the Warby Parker retail managers do? One of the very first steps is to create alignment on the metrics the company will be using. Warby Parker achieved this by creating a data dictionary. A data dictionary is a universal definition of particular metrics within a company.

When Carl joined Warby Parker to lead their data team, he found the company at a crossroads:

> It was a typical situation. [Business intelligence] was run on Excel spreadsheets. So we have lots of different business teams with lots of different spreadsheets and they had their core business logic, like what do we mean by sales channel and the product booking, embedded into those Excel spreadsheets. The problem is you have different teams using common terminology like bookings and sales channel but those definitions didn't match up.
>
> So they were talking across purposes because the numbers didn't match. And in addition, what people thought were in the spreadsheets wasn't what was actually implemented. So they didn't have some edge cases implemented.[16]

With Carl at the helm, the data team's first priority was to create a common lexicon that would help employees communicate using data. Carl and his data scientists worked with each team across the company to assemble existing metrics and define new measures, which weren't being tracked but were essential to the ongoing success of the company. When teams differed in their definitions, the data team mediated the conversations until the teams agreed upon a universal definition.

After the data team had recorded all the metrics and hashed out a single definition for each one, they created a dictionary, a Rosetta Stone, that was accessible by all employees. The dictionary contained the canonical definitions of each metric and where those data could be found.

Warby Parker teams use the company's data dictionary to educate new employees and to provide a single source of truth whenever a metric needs to be clarified. This Rosetta Stone enables productive and incisive conversations about data across teams, bolstering or refuting arguments and accelerating decisions.

But these meetings didn't stop after the dictionary was authored. Rather, the data dictionary is a living document, transforming as the

---

[16]"Look & Tell NYC: Warby Parker on Data Driven Cultures," Looker, September 29, 2015.

company evolves. When the company branches into new lines of business, develops expertise in new marketing techniques, and grows the sales team, Warby Parker will require new metrics to understand how those efforts perform relative to their goals. The data dictionary must also advance; new metrics are added and unimportant ones are deleted.

The data team at Warby Parker isn't sitting in an ivory tower using algorithms to forecast the company's revenue five years from today. Rather, these expert individuals roam the company, ensuring that employee access to important data remains unfettered and that conversations using data are free-flowing and productive. They continuously remove friction that might prevent employees from asking and answering the questions vital to decision making.

The One Equation That Defines the Business

I came across another way of developing a similar glossary at Google.

"What is the one equation that describes our business?" asked Scott, our new director at Google, during one of our first meetings. I had been there for only a few quarters, so I was startled when he asked. I had never viewed our business this way, but after he asked the question, I wondered why I hadn't. It seemed obvious in retrospect.

I was six months into a job at Google, working on the AdSense team in the Mountain View office. Tucked away in 1350 Charleston, a five-minute walk from the center of the campus, some of the world's smartest engineers were building the search engine that served billions of queries per month. The AdSense Operations team ensured the success of the hundreds of thousands of website publishers who displayed AdSense ads on their web pages to generate revenue.

What started as a simple question became a complex and insightful exercise. Over his first week or so, through many interviews like mine, Scott developed that equation for AdSense, and it filled a whiteboard.

Scott plied the equation to grasp how the business worked. He refined and polished the equation until he identified all the contributing parts to revenue. These questions led him to understand historical product-development decisions, advertiser and publisher policies, and the values of the company. They revealed the strengths of the company, but they also made it plain that many assumptions underpinning previous decisions were no longer true. Identifying those inaccuracies and correcting them unlocked tremendous revenue growth.

The equation became an important management tool in our conversations. When we discussed new projects, Scott would ask me to point on the whiteboard where the project fit within the equation—which lever the project impacted and whether the project could materially accelerate revenue growth. Boy, did it clarify priorities.

Let me walk through this simplified equation. AdSense generates revenue whenever a user clicks on an ad. So, the total revenue generated by AdSense is equal to the number of ad impressions multiplied by the click-through rate multiplied by the revenue per click.

An ad impression occurs when a user visits a website like that of the *New York Times* and sees an advertisement. The total number of ad impressions is a function of the number of web publishers running AdSense and the fraction of visitors that see an advertisement. Some publishers put ads only on certain pages or only in front of certain users.

Also, AdSense wasn't the only ad network, so we were competing against Yahoo, Microsoft, and many others for the same ad impressions. Last, having two or three ad units, slots where ads might appear, would double or triple the number of ad impressions compared to having just one ad unit.

To maximize ad impressions, the acquisitions team sought to convert more and more websites to AdSense. The acquisitions teams used all kinds of data to prioritize which customers to pursue, including the number of people visiting that website, how quickly traffic was growing on the website, and the kind of content published on the website.

In addition, account managers were tasked with preventing churn. A churned publisher is one that decides to use another ad network instead of Google. Each time we lost the customer, they took their ad impressions with them.

The click-through rate is the fraction of visitors who actually click on an ad. There are lots of different variables to contribute to this metric. The quality of the advertisements supplied by advertisers matters. In addition, the placement of the ads, whether they are on the top of the page or buried in the bottom right-hand corner, will materially impact the click-through rate. Last, the relevance of the ads to the content on the page contributes as well.

To maximize the click-through rate, the AdWords team that managed the relationships with the advertisers would share best practices with advertisers when they composed their advertisements. The AdSense operations team would work with publishers to recommend the best places to put advertisements to both maximize performance and also maintain a great user experience for the reader. And the AdSense engineering team tweaked and tuned the advertising relevancy models to continuously match the best ads with the right content.

Each time an ad is clicked, an advertiser is charged a cost per click (CPC). Three factors determine the CPC. The first is the willingness to pay specified by the advertiser. Each advertiser values a click differently based upon their business. An interested buyer for a music album is not as valuable as an in-market car shopper, so CPCs varied by industry quite widely.

Second, Google employed an auction to determine the true cost per click. Imagine three different advertisers bidding for the same click. One is willing to bid 5 cents per click, the second is willing to bid 6 cents, and the third is willing to bid 15 cents. Because Google employed a reverse auction, the third advertiser would win the auction but pay the amount bid by the second person, or 6 cents. This is to avoid the "winner's curse."

Third, Google weighted the cost of the click by the likelihood of that click actually converting into a purchase for the advertiser. Engineers would work to tune the weighting factors by publishers based upon the data we had about each website. A top-tier publisher like the *New York Times* would receive full credit for a click. But a lower-tier publisher, often called a content farm, which employs computers to automatically generate content to attract clicks and generate revenue, would suffer a discounted cost per click. Again, engineers would work to tune the weighting factors by publishers based upon the data we had about each website.

At the highest level, that's how AdSense works. And that simple equation helped us understand all of the variables that we were supposed to measure, and which ones mattered more than others. But, most of all, the equation guided our decision making.

This equation remained on Scott's office whiteboard for years. Every time I walked past his office, I would glance at that equation and smile. What an incisive management tool.

Every business has an equation that describes how it generates revenue. At the highest level, this equation can be quite simple, just like the one I've produced above for AdSense. But each variable within that equation isn't isolated. It is influenced by a series of other factors like the efforts of the engineering team or the operations team. And those processes have equations.

So we can imagine an enormous tree, starting with the highest-level equation, and leaves branching from each of the variables within those equations to get other equations that describe the contributing factors to those second-degree variables. And so on.

Data-driven companies strive to develop these equations and manage the business by them. Within these equations, the key variables are the things to measure, the very same metrics found within the data dictionary. These are the numbers that matter.

Like a baton in a relay race, data must be transitioned between teams seamlessly. At Warby Parker, the data team facilitates these handoffs by creating a single data dictionary with a consistent definition, so the sales team understands precisely how the marketing team determines lead quality and lead volume. Those lead volumes coupled with the sales team's conversion rates determine the bookings and growth of the business.

Equations like the one Scott derived at Google and data dictionaries like the one Carl's team hewed at Warby Parker serve the same purpose: to provide a single language of communication across teams.

Brutal Intellectual Honesty: Speaking Data to Power

The truth is like a lion. You don't have to defend it. Let it loose. It will defend itself.

—St. Augustine

Dominic Orr, former CEO of Aruba Networks, champions a unique management philosophy he calls brutal intellectual honesty. "If you asked me to distill the formula for success to one factor

I would say it is speed. That is speed of execution. Speed of innovation."[17] For Orr, brutal intellectual honesty is axiomatic, an unquestionable tenet of successful, decisive teams. Orr expounded his philosophy in an interview with Fast Company:[18]

> Brutal intellectual honesty. We've distilled that companywide philosophy into a few simple rules. We focus on collecting as many facts as quickly as we can, and then we decide on the best, but not necessarily the perfect, solution. Think Socratic method at the speed of light.
>
> There's no silent disagreement, and no getting personal, and definitely no "let's take it offline" mentality. Our goal is to make each major decision in a single meeting. People arrive with a proposal or a solution, and with the facts to support it. After an idea is presented, we open the floor to objective, and often withering, critiques. And if the idea collapses under scrutiny, we move on to another: no hard feelings. We're judging the idea, not the person.
>
> At the same time, we don't really try to regulate emotions. Passionate conflict means that we're getting somewhere, not that the discussion is out of control. But one person does act as referee, by asking basic questions like "Is this good for the customer?" or "Does it keep our time-to-market advantage intact?" By focusing relentlessly on the facts, we're able to see the strengths and weaknesses of an idea clearly and quickly.

To be brutally honest, we must dissociate ideas and ego. When we mix passion, data, and ideas with ego, we become attached to ideas and positions and reasons why we should pursue a particular path.

These mixed motives generate friction, and inevitably stonewall meetings. Once we've committed to a position, we cannot retrench and save face, lest we suffer a bruised ego. So, the conversations become political or emotional, and the conversation no longer focuses on the key issue at hand, but on how individuals within the room maintain their self-perceptions. All of this siphons time away from execution and progress.

---

[17]Dominic Orr, "Competing with Giants: It's All about Speed," *Stanford eCorner*, October 17, 2007. Retrieved from http://ecorner.stanford.edu/authorMaterialInfo.html?mid=1864
[18]C. Olofson, "So Many Decisions, So Little Time," *Fast Company*, September 30, 1999. Retrieved from www.fastcompany.com/37743/so-many-decisions-so-little-

As Orr explains, inculcating brutal intellectual honesty into a team requires a self-confident team, assured enough in front of their peers to suggest ideas, support an argument with data, hear the idea criticized, defend it, and finally select the best idea among the alternatives dispassionately to determine which idea is best.

Pixar also employs brutal intellectual honesty to consistently create category-defining movies. Pixar started life as the Computer Graphics Lab of the New York Institute of Technology in 1974. A group of graduate students financed by Dr. Alexander Schure sought to create the first 90-minute movie entirely generated by computers. The resources the project consumed quickly outstripped the university's budget, and George Lucas, the founder of Lucasfilm, offered to hire the department. Lucas recruited six of the graduate students, including the head of the computer graphics lab, Edwin Catmull. Six years later, Lucasfilm ran into financial difficulty and sought to sell the computer graphics group. Steve Jobs lowballed the process with a $10 million offer, but he was the only bidder, and after much deliberation, George Lucas accepted.

For the next 10 years, Pixar built and marketed top-of-the-line computer graphics workstations to movie studios. But the computers didn't sell. To keep the lights on, Pixar sold service contracts, generating computer animation for studios including Disney. On the brink of bankruptcy, Catmull signed a joint venture with Disney, which would invest $26 million to jointly produce *Toy Story*. It was a bet-the-company-move. The cash infusion helped, but Pixar needed more than the Disney contract would supply. Jobs, who had continued to finance the company until this point, was reticent to invest more in Pixar. He cajoled Catmull and the rest of the leadership to file for IPO a week after *Toy Story* was to debut. If the film flopped, so would the IPO, and the company would fold.

On November 22, 1995, *Toy Story* premiered to wide acclaim. The first 90-minute computer-generated film, *Toy Story* met huge success in movie theaters globally, and would eventually gross $361 million. Considered perhaps the finest animated film ever made, *Toy Story* catapulted Pixar's share price at IPO by 77 percent. Saved by their creativity and flush with cash, Pixar began development of several new movies, including a sequel to their blockbuster.

As the company prospered, Catmull and others began to manage multiple studios producing different movies. Over time, they created a team within the company to evaluate the status of each these studios and guide them to success. They called it the Braintrust.

Ed Catmull explained, "To understand what the Braintrust does, and why it is so central to Pixar, you have to start with the basic truth: people who take on complicated creative projects become lost at some point in the process. It is the nature of things—in order to create you must internalize and almost become the project for a while, and that near-fusing with the project is an essential part of its emergence. But it is also confusing."[19]

As Catmull describes in his chronicle of Pixar, *Creativity, Inc.*, the Braintrust has two important qualities. First, the people composing the Braintrust all have produced a great story. The mutual respect conferred by fellow directors and storytellers creates the environment of deep trust. Second, the Braintrust has no authority. They cannot force or compel a team to accept their feedback. The Braintrust is responsible for delivering brutal intellectual honesty, a discipline that has fueled Pixar's continuing success across 16 feature films that have grossed on average more than $600 million and in total about $10 billion.

Brutal intellectual honesty aims to slay the HIPPO, or the highest-paid person's opinion, as the determining factor of the direction of a project, team, or company. Left unmitigated, this management artifact wreaks disastrous consequences on companies.

The heralded architect of the Apple Store, Ron Johnson, revolutionized retail for Apple. Since the first store opened on May 15, 2001, in Tyson's Corner, Virginia, Apple Stores have blossomed to more than 450 globally. What's more, according to a *Fortune* analysis, Apple Stores generate more revenue per square foot than any other marque. In 2015, Apple Stores produced $4,798 in sales per square foot, nearly 50 percent more than second-place Tiffany's, at $3,132.[20]

---

[19] Edwin E. Catmull and Amy Wallace, *Creativity, Inc.: Overcoming the Unseen Forces That Stand in the Way of True Inspiration* (New York: Random House, 2014). eBook edition Location 1435.
[20] P. Wahba, "Apple Extends Lead in U.S. Top 10 Retailers by Sales per Square Foot," *Fortune*, March 13, 2015. Retrieved from http://fortune.com/2015/03/13/apples-holiday-top-10-retailers-iphone/.

Selected by the J.C. Penney board of directors to lead a transformation at the ailing retailer, Johnson did not fare well. Noel Tichy, professor at the Ross School of Business at the University of Michigan, asserts the lack of data-driven decision making reduced J.C. Penney's value by more than 50 percent in 18 months.

> Arriving with a $52 million package, Johnson was certainly the highest paid person at JC Penney.... When making changes, Johnson trusted his gut rather than the data in front of him. Although he was reportedly shown focus group results clearly indicating consumer's strong preference for discounts, Johnson pressed ahead with his changes, mandating a fixed pricing matrix for all merchants to follow. The ensuing confusion and consumer defections were at the heart company's 25 percent sales drop. But Johnson didn't stop there—he not only ignored existing data, but he was also convinced he didn't need new information to validate the righteousness of his strategy.[21]

Because the customer base, the product, the market, and the team of each company are unique, managers cannot simply replicate a successful formula from a previous company and blindly apply it to another business. What got you here won't get you there. This is true at every level of management, from the CEO to a team lead.

Each business must approach the market to maximize its strengths and seize its opportunities. Leaders who understand this important principle also recognize that data is the basis of discovering the right go-to-market for each company.

Data-based decision-making leaders recognize that great ideas don't always come from the most experienced or most senior person in the room. Great ideas can originate from anywhere. And often data is the best way to ensure those ideas rise the ranks.

Not stopping with just internal ideas, a few innovative companies have been soliciting customers and experts outside the company to suggest transformational ideas.

---

[21]C. DeRose and N. Tichy, "What Happens When a 'HiPPO' Runs Your Company?," *Forbes*, April 15, 2013. Retrieved from www.forbes.com/sites/derosetichy/2013/04/15/what-happens-when-a-hippo-runs-your-company/.

Allstate, the $24 billion Illinois-based insurer founded in 1931, has developed risk models for predicting the profitability of the business for nearly 100 years. In 2014, the company sought to improve its ability to forecast bodily injury claims in car accidents. Predict too many accidents and the company leaves profits on the table by quoting very high rates, causing potential customers to look elsewhere. Predict too few, and Allstate must insure higher-risk drivers and pay the price of more frequent and expensive accidents.

Allstate supplied the problem and an anonymized data set from 2005 to 2007 to Kaggle, a company that operates data science competitions and has built a community of thousands of data scientists globally. Allstate provided a $10,000 prize for the top three entrants. MIT Sloan School professor Andrew McAfee described the experiment a bit further:

> *"Allstate took some of its data, made it available for one of these data science competitions, and said, 'Hey, can you beat our current best prediction for which of these cars is going to get into an accident somewhere down the road?' Sure enough, the data scientist could beat the baseline prediction by a lot."* [22]

Over the next 90 days, 202 data scientists submitted close to 1,300 different algorithms to Allstate that considered correlations among engine horsepower, car length, number of cylinders, and other vehicle characteristics. Matthew Carle, an actuary in Australia, won the prize. In just three months, he had developed a new algorithm that improved Allstate's predictive capability by a staggering 340 percent. [23]

Sometimes, a new set of eyes on a problem reveals a fundamentally new approach that transforms the scope and scale of the solution. That's why brutal intellectual honesty matters.

[22] D. Gallagher, "The Decline of the HIPPO (Highest Paid Person's Opinion)," *MIT Sloan Management Review*, April 1, 2012. Retrieved from http://sloanreview.mit.edu/article/the-decline-of-the-hppo-highest-paid-persons-opinion.

[23] J. Sandman, "Allstate Taps the Crowd to Predict Insurance Claims," *U.S. News and World Report*, May 15, 2012. Retrieved from http://money.usnews.com/money/business-economy/articles/2012/05/15/allstate-taps-the-crowd-to-predict-insurance-claims.

Putting Pride in Its Place: How Data Transforms Cultures

We are proud when we identify ourselves with an imaginary self, a leader, a holy cause, a collective body of possessions. There is fear and intolerance in pride; it is insensitive and uncompromising.

—Bruce Lee

Startup.com, a 2001 documentary directed by D.A. Pennebaker, an Oscar-winning filmmaker, recounts the brief life of the dot-com startup govWorks, a New York City company founded in 1998 and headquartered in a sparse, airy loft on Franklin Street in eastern Tribeca. Founders Kaleil Isaza Tuzman and Tom Herman raised more than $70 million to build software that enabled citizens to pay municipalities for parking tickets, apply for jobs, and discover community information online.

The documentary opens with the founder, Tom, a thirty-something, bearded, and spectacled computer scientist, outfitted in a tan sharkskin suit and purple iridescent tie, announcing a new CEO to the eight-person company. Kaleil is a high school friend of Tom's. He has just quit Goldman Sachs's technology, media, and telecom team after four years. Still looking the part of a banker in a light blue suit, checked azure shirt with matching pocket square, and heavy Swiss watch, the imposing Kaleil opens his full-grain leather briefcase and addresses the company. As he dusts off the Office Depot box he uses for his chair, Kaleil proclaims, "This is the beginning of a great thing," to employees' applause.

That evening, the executive team, now alone at Kaleil's posh apartment, registers the domain name govWorks.com and celebrate with high-fives. But, 10 minutes later, Kaleil reveals his hesitation about the name. He's not sure it's the moniker of a billion-dollar company. The naming debate begins.

Around midnight, the three founders walk to a local pizzeria. Kaleil prompts a patron, "Should the company be called govWorks or NextTown?" Later that night Kaleil proposes a third name, Unto Caesar. "Hi, Mr. Mayor, my name is Kaleil, and I'm calling to sell you a $2 million systems integration software. I'm from UntoCaesar," the head of engineering chides. Back and forth, back and forth, the executive teams bats the pros and cons of each idea.

After more time deliberating, Kaleil resolves to meditate on the name. Twenty minutes later, he returns triumphantly, beaming with pride, and proclaims to his team: "I did what I do before every major decision in my life and that is sit and meditate. And I decided that we are govWorks!"

This is how millions of decisions are made every year in big and small companies: lots of opinionated debate followed by the most senior person ultimately selecting the path forward. While sometimes it's critical to make decisions without any data, most of the time data can easily be collected to support the decision.

Today, the govWorks founding team might run a small-scale advertising campaign on Google or Facebook to benchmark different domain names. Which domain name has the highest click-through rate on ads? They might run a survey on SurveyMonkey to poll a thousand potential customers to understand the brand sensitivities of their target market. Each of these experiments might take a few days, but ultimately the management team would have a better sense of their customer before making a decision.

Opinions may change on a daily basis depending on the mood in the room, the effectiveness of one person's argument, politics behind the scenes, the time of day, and any number of other, invisible factors. GovWorks may have been called UntoCaesar if Kaleil had meditated in a different mood. The decision is quite arbitrary.

In addition, this decision-making caprice engenders pride in the person who has decided the matter for his team. There is no way to defend the decision other than an opinion. When asked to justify the choice, the decision maker doesn't have much evidence to bolster the position other than his intuition. So, a review of a previous decision frequently devolves from a set of basic questions into an ad hominem attack, a questioning of the decision maker's individual abilities. Backed into a corner with his competence in question, this decision maker will defend the decision irrationally and fiercely to protect his reputation, even if the decision is plainly the wrong one. This is pride, an irrational attachment to a particular decision.

Data is the antidote to this toxic manner of deciding. We have consistently observed that the very best companies create repeatable decision-making practices. Given the same data, a company should make the same decision each time, unbiased by the invisible factors of one person's opinion or the dynamics of the day.

Imagine the govWorks naming meeting consisting of reviewing data from the advertising test and the survey. The team would gather around a collection of charts, each offering their own interpretation of the data and collaborating toward the conclusion. And because the data is plain for everyone to see, anyone within the meeting can point out an observation that could change the trajectory of the meeting and defend it. You can't do that with opinions.

The leader who ultimately determines the final name of the company can step through the team's rationale at any point in the future and defend the position with more than just an opinion. Future debate over the naming decision revolves around the data rather than individuals. Did we collect the right data? Did we analyze the data well? What can we learn in the future about the way that we make these kinds of decisions? All of these are positive questions that help the company improve its operations.

Suddenly, all of the pride and defensiveness necessary to make and defend decisions dissipates. Gone is the fear of changing direction in the future. Why did the product team decide to change the logo color from red to violet? Not because of the whim of a new VP of product, but because of better customer data indicating the new color scheme will improve sales.

Google has earned a reputation for relentlessly experimenting with new products and refining existing products by assessing tens of variations to determine exactly which performs best. Google displays ads on many of its properties including Google.com and Gmail.com. Managing director of Google UK Dan Cobley described how the company experimented with those colors and the massive consequence.

> In the world of the hippo [the highest-paid person's opinion], you ask the chief designer or the marketing director to pick a blue and that's the solution. In the world of data you can run experiments to find the right answer.
>
> We ran "1%" experiments, showing 1% of users one blue, and another experiment showing 1% another blue. And actually, to make sure we covered all our bases, we ran forty other experiments showing all the shades of blue you could possibly imagine. And we saw which shades of blue people liked the most, demonstrated by how much they clicked on them. As a result we learned that a slightly purpler

shade of blue was more conducive to clicking than a slightly greener shade of blue, and gee whizz, we made a decision.

But the implications of that for us, given the scale of our business, was that we made an extra $200m a year in ad revenue.[24]

When we use data to determine how a team should move forward, there is no pride in that decision. There is no long-term attachment to an idea that the team leader championed. When we make decisions with data, we decide collectively because we're all evaluating the facts and interpreting them as a team.

This changes the culture within a team. Anyone can contribute an idea, an interpretation, a new data point that reveals a new perspective to the team. Quickly, team meetings become far more collaborative sessions focused on extracting all the insight from the available data and asking questions about what other data should be collected. More data brings new perspectives, which helps the team further improve their decision-making process and performance.

And more importantly, the repeatability of the decision-making process removes pride from the conversation. The team owns the decision, not just the team's leader. That's how data transforms a company's culture.

---

[24] Alex Hern, "Why Google Has 200M Reasons to Put Engineers over Designers," *The Guardian*, February 5, 2014.

Chapter 5

Five Steps to Creating a Data-Driven Company—From Recruiting to Regression, It All Starts with Curiosity: Changing the Culture

It All Starts with Curiosity

The first and simplest emotion which we discover in the human mind, is curiosity.

—Edmund Burke

How does one change a company's culture to become more data-driven? It all starts with curiosity. Curiosity is an innate characteristic, and a marvelous, empowering attribute. We learn only when we have both the curiosity to ask a question and the tools to answer it. To change our cultures, we should celebrate and reward curiosity.

A Swiss developmental psychologist who lived from 1896 to 1980, Jean Piaget is widely regarded as one of the great pioneers of understanding how humans learn. A gifted boy, Piaget began attending meetings of the Friends of Nature Club, a group of biologists from the local university in Neuchâtel, who read academic papers. He published his first paper at age 10 on the topic of an albino sparrow.

As he matured, Piaget evolved from biology to human psychology. He developed the theory of genetic epistemology, which proposed that learning is an ongoing process of invention and reinvention as we interact with our world.

Piaget studied children. He explained how children learn about the existence of numbers.

[Piaget] famously argued that children are neither taught nor born with the understanding that number is an abstract property; rather, they discover it. In one classic example, he described a child who, playing with collection of small stones, realized that no matter how he arranged them (straight line, circle, or scattered), the number of stones remained unchanged. Through the child's own impulse to examine the stones and test out different possibilities with them, he learned a crucial principle of abstract thinking: the conservation of number.[1]

When presented with something new, we assimilate the new bit of data: The number of stones is constant. Next, we accommodate the new information by modifying our existing worldview to incorporate the new event. The number of stones is constant regardless of how I arrange the stones. Last, we realize shortcomings in our way of viewing the world and seek to rationalize the new data point with our old model, discovering a new mental model, which Piaget called equilibration: Conservation of number must be true with stones as much as marbles, cupcakes, and toy cars. Those are the three key steps to learning: accommodate, assimilate, and equilibrate.

Employees within the company at every level must crave an explanation and develop the ability to explain trends to other people, make sense of them, and change the company's direction based on the new insights. Empowered by data, these workers can then create hypotheses, design experiments to test them, and validate or invalidate the idea. That's when the cycle of learning begins.

Why You Should Stop Listening to Your Boss

Innovative teams accommodate, assimilate, and equilibrate new information hundreds of times per year. Data-driven companies want every employee to discover new information, understand it within the context of their existing frameworks, determine what assumptions are no longer true, and then evolve the way they think about the world to move things forward. When we do that, we harness the power of curiosity and transform it into innovation.

---

[1] Susan Engel, "Children's Need to Know: Curiosity in Schools," *Harvard Educational Review* 81, no. 4 (2011): 625–645.

This starts a tiny snowball rolling, and the curiosity becomes infectious. People start asking questions themselves. What does that analysis say about my performance? What would that report tell me about my customers? How can we be doing better? How does this change in the industry impact our team, our business?

In an interview with Fast Company called "Why Intuit Founder Scott Cook Wants You to Stop Listening to Your Boss," Scott Cook, founder and CEO of Intuit, articulated the benefits of a data-driven culture rife with experimentation. Founded 32 years ago and now worth more than $26 billion, Intuit sells software, including TurboTax, Quicken, and Mint, that millions of consumers and small businesses trust to manage their finances and pay taxes.[2]

Cook explains:

> Three things happen. One, you make better decisions because it's actually real consumers or real production methods that aren't based on theory or PowerPoint. . . .
>
> Two, you enable your most junior people to test their best ideas, and when you're doing PowerPoint presentations, whose ideas are most likely to get lost?
>
> The third is, you get surprises more often, and surprises are a key source of innovation. You only get a surprise when you're trying something and the result is different than you expected, so the sooner you run the experiment the sooner you're likely to find a surprise and surprise is the market speaking to you, telling you something you didn't know. Several of our businesses [at Intuit] came out of surprises.

Cook articulates three fundamental cultural shifts. First, a company begins to use data to decide. Instead of conjecture, observations and experimental studies furnish debaters with data to argue and determine the right path forward.

Second, teams collect the best ideas from everyone in a room. One of the most important consequences of becoming a data-driven organization is that anyone in the company can contribute a trajectory-altering idea and defend it with data. This is empowering

---

[2]S. Cook, "Why Intuit Founder Scott Cook Wants You to Stop Listening to Your Boss," *Fast Company*, October 28, 2013. Retrieved from www.fastcompany.com/3020699/bottom-line/why-intuit-founder-scott-cook-wants-you-to-stop-listening-to-your-boss.

and addictive. It puts the onus on people with great ideas to research, explore, and argue their ideas. Suddenly, team members can influence their project's trajectory.

In addition, this type of collaboration invites meritocracy. If truly the best ideas rise to the surface, and everyone in the room knows who generated the ideas, credit will go where it is due.

Third, data encourages experimentation and surprises. Surprises foster new ways of thinking. They challenge the establishment. When dogged with opinions or knee-jerk answers of "that's why we've always done it," we all can feel disenfranchised. Data pushes us to experiment. How do customers react when I e-mail them eight hours after we've spoken instead of 24 hours? How does conversion rate change with News Gothic font compared to Helvetica on the home page? Will more leads convert to customers if I use the Coca-Cola or the Caterpillar equipment case study? And with the data from the experiment, employees can enact the change they wish to see in their business, which reinforces these three positive behaviors.

Later in the interview, Cook discusses how Eric Ries's Lean Startup methodology changed Intuit's product-development methods.

In 2004, after Ries graduated from Yale with a degree in computer science, he started a virtual world company, There. It would fold, but Ries reincarnated the vision in a new company called IMVU, which operates a virtual world, complete with a fully functional economy, for millions of users. As of 2013, the company generates more than $55 million year in revenue and is profitable.[3]

Steve Blank, a well-known Silicon Valley entrepreneur and professor at the University of California business school, invested in IMVU on the condition that the founders would attend his entrepreneurship class. Inspired by Blank's teachings in those classes, Eric began to develop the Lean Startup methodology, a way of building software companies based on the manufacturing techniques of the Toyota Production System.

Lean Startup methods instruct team leaders to develop hypotheses, determine success metrics ahead of time, research the idea with users, and test the idea using experiments. Lean Startup reduces the cycle time to discovery of great ideas.

---

[3]"IMVU Inc. Celebrates Nine Years of Connecting People Around the World, Expands Profitable Business to Mobile," press release, IMVU Information, April 8, 2013.

Intuit acquired a payroll company called Paycycle. As Intuit discovered after the acquisition, many new Paycycle customers enroll on the day they would like to send paychecks to employees. But the software requires these businesses to set up their accounts by filling out data like the Social Security numbers of employees, tax status, current payments to the employee, and benefits data. All this setup requires 24 to 48 hours for the business to complete before it can issue paychecks.

An Intuit engineer wondered if a feature enabling businesses to cut checks immediately might improve conversion rates. He created some basic wireframe drawings of what the new user interface might resemble. Then he performed some basic user research. Not a single one of 20 customers polled thought they would use the feature. Twenty opinions all saying the same thing: Don't build this feature.

But, Cook describes, "Eric looked at it and said, 'Why don't you run an experiment tomorrow. Just put up the option [in the software]. Show prospects the choices, and let's see what they pick. Don't build it yet. Just show them choices, and if they pick the paychecks first, setup second, we say, "So sorry, we haven't built it yet," and give them a $100 gift certificate.'"

Fifty-eight percent of the new customers clicked on the option to issue paychecks right then. The data disproved the opinions of 20 customers. So the engineers built the feature. As Cook says, "Now, our payroll division is going to have their fastest growth in 10 years because of an experiment. Without the experimentation stuff, it never would have happened."

The most innovative companies are the ones who find great ideas through experiments and push them into production. Experimentation is at the core of that innovation because it equips employees, even the most junior within a company, to support their argument with data. That's the data empowerment that matters.

We have found that engendering this culture starts with curiosity: hiring people who possess it, rewarding people who embody it, and cultivating it. By setting the tone for how decisions will be made, how new projects will be chosen, how meetings must be run, and how employees will be evaluated, the management of forward-thinking companies reinforces the cycle on a daily basis. This fundamental change all starts with hiring curious people.

How to Recruit Curious People

Maia Josebachvilli's love of skydiving led her to a career as VP of people and strategy at Greenhouse. In college, Maia couldn't afford to skydive frequently, so she organized groups of friends to jump from planes, both for fun and to negotiate the group discounts that enabled her to skydive for free. Since then, Maia has completed more than 750 skydives.

After graduating from Dartmouth College, Maia traded derivatives for a few years. Pining for the outdoors, she quit her Wall Street career to found Urban Escapes. Urban Escapes whisked young urbanites on exotic and exhilarating excursions, such as rafting trips complete with riverside barbecues and beer tasting at local breweries, and a seven-day trek in Costa Rica that included mountain biking across the active Turrialba volcano and ziplining across several miles of lush rain forest canopy.

Started in the throes of the 2008 recession, Urban Escapes thrived until it was acquired by LivingSocial in 2010. The opportunity left Maia to pursue her love of travel. She and her husband departed on a year-long round-the-world sabbatical. They hiked the Fox Glacier in New Zealand, volunteered in a remote hospital in Bhutan, and shared meals with the Kalahari Bushmen of Namibia.

When Maia returned to the United States, she joined Greenhouse, a flourishing young New York City company that develops recruiting software. Founded in 2012 by Daniel Chait and Jon Stross to solve the team-building challenges they faced at previous companies, Greenhouse brings together many innovations and important advances in the world of recruiting, including A/B testing of job requisitions and standardized interview rubrics. Maia's unusual background afforded her a new perspective on the business of recruiting talent, a process very few companies do well.

According to Adam Grant, a professor of organizational behavior at Wharton, most interviews are a waste of time. The typical job interview accounts for only 8 percent of the differences in the performance and productivity of employees.[4] Most interviews aren't

---

[4]A. Grant, "What's Wrong with Job Interviews, and How to Fix Them," LinkedIn, June 10, 2013. Retrieved from https://www.linkedin.com/pulse/20130610025112-69244073-will-smart-companies-interview-your-kids.

structured properly. Interviewers rush into candidate meetings without having prepared. The candidate reviews his resume and responds to questions that pop into the mind of the interviewer during the 45-minute meeting. It's no surprise that these haphazard interviews yield no insight into the ultimate success of the candidate in the role.

Instead of these slapdash interactions, Grant advocates companies employ a clear, structured process:

1. Establish the characteristics of the ideal candidate at the outset of a search process.
2. Before the team interviews candidates, the hiring manager and the recruiter write questions that will establish whether a candidate embodies those characteristics.
3. The interviewing team scores each candidate on a consistent numerical scale across these attributes.
4. The candidate with the highest aggregate score is hired.

Greenhouse has embedded Grant's philosophy into its software to ensure a consistent and more effective recruiting process, one that results in hiring an employee who is more likely to succeed on the job. Mis-hires, hiring people who aren't a good fit for a role, can cost a company between 14 and 28 times the employee's base salary, calculating the time spent recruiting the person, the opportunity cost of not hiring a better candidate, the costs of transitioning the person out of the company, and the costs of hiring a replacement.

Advances like Greenhouse's structured interviewing process advance the recruiting practices across industries. Using Greenhouse software, well-run recruiting teams staff their companies with more successful candidates. Maia is a key part of that revolution. As we've seen, her background isn't typical for a head of human resources. But her experiences as a former CEO, trader, and company builder give her a radically different lens through which to view the recruiting function.

Maia has observed recruiting patterns in hundreds of companies. From that experience, she has developed best practices for recruiting with metrics. With Greenhouse's panoptic view of those companies, Maia has established that talent acquisition teams using analytics are two times more likely to improve the success of their recruiting efforts and three times more likely to improve their efficiency and reduce costs.

Maia's predilection for data has pushed her to establish a set of five strategic recruiting metrics, which she reports to the Greenhouse executive team each quarter.[5] These metrics resemble the diagnostics that many sales teams use to understand the sales funnel, and they provide similar visibility into the efforts and successes of the hiring team.

Qualified candidates (QCs): The equivalent of a sales qualified lead, a QC is defined as a phone interview that qualifies a candidate as a good fit for a job requisition. The QC is a leading indicator of whether the team will attain its hiring goals. By understanding the ratio of QC to accepted offer rate over time, a company can forecast the odds of attaining its hiring goal that quarter, just as sales teams estimate bookings. QC metrics answer questions like: How is the recruiting team developing a large candidate pipeline? Which candidate acquisition channels work best? How much does it cost for the company to hire a candidate?

Days to close: Speed is a competitive advantage in recruiting, because the most sought-after candidates typically have many competing offers. Greenhouse maintains less than 30 days of latency between first contact and signed offer. Across Greenhouse's 1,000-plus customers, the average time to close is 42 days.

Candidate satisfaction: After every interview, Greenhouse sends a survey to candidates to gauge their satisfaction with the process, including how well the position was explained, how well prepared the interviewers were, and whether they felt respected and were treated courteously. The top businesses attain a satisfaction rate of 70 percent or better.

Offer acceptance rate: What fraction of people who receive offers accept them? This figure should be quite high, 75 percent, or greater in some cases. If the offer acceptance rate is low, the recruiting team should investigate. Some causes include lower candidate

---

[5]M. Josebachvili, "Recruiting Metrics—Strategic and Tactical KPIs for Talent Acquisition," September 10, 2015. Retrieved from www.slideshare.net/Josebachvili/recruiting-metrics-strategic-and-tactical-kpis-for-talent-acquisition.

satisfaction, an unduly long hiring cycle, unclear hiring parameters in the job requisition, and miscommunication between recruiting and hiring managers.

Hires to goal: Divide the total number of new hires by the hiring goal. If a company isn't achieving its hires-to-goal number, it should investigate the obstacles, whether in sourcing talent, in the evaluation process, or in the actual offer. This metric raises these questions: Is the recruiting team consistently able to hire people according to the board-approved hiring plan? If not, what can be done to put the team back on track? Where in the recruiting funnel is the team challenged? Is it qualified candidates? Is it the conversion rate from telephone screens to in-person interviews? Or could it be the offer acceptance rate? What are the implications for compensation structure?

This simple scorecard of five metrics provides a wealth of information and data to a business's management team, who can understand whether the company-building efforts are on track. It also instills a discipline and rigor within the recruiting team.

In addition, these metrics inform a company's financial planning. If a business has a benchmark for the performance of its recruiting team, the company can understand precisely the number of increased recruiters necessary to attain the year's hiring goals. And, the company can evaluate the effectiveness of recruiters by comparing an individual recruiter's performance to that of his peers. If a recruiter is outperforming, sourcing a much larger quantity of qualified candidates, the company can be confident they have hired a terrific recruiter.

Equally important to measuring the conversion funnel from qualified candidate to employee is establishing precisely who the right candidate for a roll might be. Before a funnel is developed, the hiring manager and the company broadly must both understand the characteristics of the idea hire.

The performance/culture matrix shown in Figure 5.1 is an invaluable tool for evaluating candidates. This 2×2 matrix plots where hires for a company should be: only in the top-right quadrant, which is both a high-performing person and a good cultural fit. The performance/culture matrix is as applicable to a 10,000-person enterprise as it is to a 5-person team.

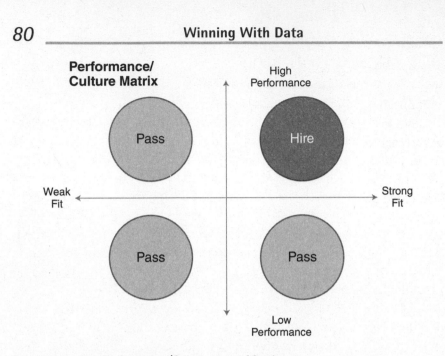

FIGURE 5.1   The Performance/Culture 2 × 2 Matrix

Many recruiting teams wonder how best to define culture. It can be an amorphous and intangible concept. Nevertheless, culture definition is an essential part of building a successful recruiting process.

To define a culture, follow these steps.

First, assign a culture lead, often a key member of the management team. The lead solicits feedback from current employees about what they like and don't like about working at the company, either by interviews or surveys.

Then, the culture lead condenses feedback into an initial set of values to be reviewed by the management team. The values should most strongly reflect the positives of the business, but they should also include some aspirational values to slowly evolve the culture of the company in a positive direction.

Next, the culture lead and management team present this first draft of values to the rest of the company and begin a back-and-forth dialogue. This interactive refinement process continues until consensus is reached that the values written down truly reflect the way employees feel about the company.

Last, the values become an integral component of the interview and recruiting process for new people. They form the basis of a series of structured interview questions meant to gauge the person's values and how strongly aligned he is with the rest of the employee population.

At Google, we called the collection of these values Googliness. Laszlo Bock, chief people officer at Google, described a Googley person as "curious, quick-learning generalists who can master whatever challenges are thrown at them."[6]

When I was at Google and interviewing product-management candidates, I was sent an electronic form to fill out after the interview across four categories: technical proficiency, communication skills, product insight, and Googliness. Google values cultural fit as highly as being able to write an algorithm to find the number of Fibonacci numbers less than n.

To determine cultural fit at Google, we asked behavioral questions. Behavioral interview questions test values best. If your company prizes customer-centricity in account executives, invite candidates, "Tell me about a time when you went out of your way to help a customer." After they've responded, follow up with, "Now tell me about a second time." Candidates who truly do embody customer-centricity shouldn't be challenged by these questions, and the cultural fit will become clear.

Behavioral interview questions can be hard to develop. They take a lot of effort and thinking. So, Google's talent team developed qDroid, a website for interviewers to find incisive behavioral questions. An interviewer logs into qDroid and enters the role he will be interviewing for, and qDroid provides questions he should ask in the interview that are highly correlated with a candidate's success in the role. This database is constantly being updated and the questions improved.

In addition to behavioral questions, interviews should include situational interview questions like "How would you build a list of potential customers?" These are meant to illuminate the candidate's critical thinking.

The candidate's answers to both these behavioral and situational questions, combined with an evaluation of the other desired attributes

---

[6]George Anders, "Google's People Chief, Laszlo Bock, Explains How to Hire Right," *Forbes*, October 21, 2014.

of the hire, determine where he fits in the performance/culture 2×2 matrix depicted in Figure 5.1. As Maia says, companies should hire only candidates that fit in the upper-right quadrant, who are both high performers and strong cultural fits.

This type of structured interview should test for the values the company has enumerated and will ensure a more consistent hiring success rate and better candidate fit.

As Laszlo Bock wrote in his book *Work Rules!*, Google takes metrics one step further than most companies. It collects data at every step of the interviewing process to provide interviewers feedback on their candidate judgment. Bock observes, "Every interviewer sees a record of the interview scores they have given in the past and whether those people were hired or not. This lets the interviewer know if they are correctly assessing potential Googlers, nudging them to look back at their prior notes and learn from whey they spotted or missed."[7]

This feedback cycle is critically important, especially in companies that hire hundreds or thousands of people annually, and consequently have enough data points to generate statistically meaningful results. Interviewers can pinpoint exactly where they are aligned with the company's interviewing values and where they might need training. Over time, this learning cycle improves the accuracy, predictability, consistency, and effectiveness for recruiting.

Both top-down and bottom-up change require hiring the right kinds of people, people who value curiosity. A reluctant layer of middle management within a company will stymie a data-driven culture just as effectively as an apathetic CEO. To build a curious team, develop a comprehensive set of values, recruit candidates who fit in the top-right quadrant of the performance/culture matrix, structure interview questions to assess cultural fit, and develop a recruiting funnel instrumented by the five metrics above.

---

[7]Laszlo Bock *Work Rules! Insights from Inside Google That Will Transform How You Live and Lead* (S.l.: John Murray Ltd., 2015), 104.

Chapter 6

From Hacks to Harmony: The Typical Progression of Data-Driven Companies

All of this latent curiosity brewing in a company's teams will precipitate a slew of questions that must be answered with data. As the mass of questions increases the pressure of the data team to respond, companies progress through four stages of data sophistication.

Twilio provides the communications API that enables phones, messaging, and voiceover IP to be embedded into web, desktop, and mobile software. Developers all over the world use Twilio's software to help users connect. The company was founded by Jeff Lawson, Evan Cooke, and John Walthius in 2007 in Seattle and San Francisco. Twilio has raised more than $200 million in venture capital, and as of February 2015, more than 560,000 developers use the service.

Using Twilio, developers can dynamically buy telephone numbers for calling and sending text messages. Whenever an Uber passenger calls a driver to coordinate a pickup, he uses Twilio. When a Home Depot customer asks for a general contractor referral to help him with his shelving, Home Depot's Red Beacon uses Twilio to match the customer with a trusted service provider. Even Coca-Cola uses Twilio to dispatch field technicians to repair ailing vending machines. As more and more communication moves to mobile phones, Twilio has become the switchboard for millions of conversations, text messages, and transactions globally.

Twilio's position in the ecosystem affords it a global view of the ecosystem of application developers, telephone carriers, and users.

From this vantage point, Twilio can record metadata about telephone numbers, call volumes, and text message frequency. This rich data set informs many different teams across the company, including financial reporting, engineering (performance, reliability, quality), carrier analysis, and marketing sales and product.

At the hub of the company's data, the Twilio data team empowers hundreds of employees to answer their questions as quickly as possible. Like many other companies, the Twilio data team evolved in three phases.

Step 1: Ask Your Friend, the Engineer

At the outset of the company, computer engineers designed and built the data systems. They were the only ones with the requisite knowledge and passwords to the data. So, early employees asked these engineers for data favors: Could you send me this data sometime soon, if you have a free moment?

Without a formal process, the engineer and the requester often miscommunicated. The query would need to be rewritten several times. Sometimes, the data request wasn't a single request but an ongoing one. How are revenues performing each week? In addition to the queries, engineers would write bespoke dashboards that automatically updated the data.

Quickly, the company realized this method sapped its engineering team of valuable time to build the features that would command revenue in the market and propel the company forward. Nor were employees getting the answers they needed.

Step 2: Bastardize an Existing Solution

Someone at the company suggested using Salesforce to solve Twilio's needs. The sales team was using Salesforce to run reports on their performance. Perhaps the rest of the company could use the same system if the data team uploaded the right data.

The data team wrote custom software to pipe disparate data and shoehorn it into Salesforce's database schema. Because of the complexity of Salesforce's API and the constraints on data throughput, not all the data would fit.

As business users found out later, Salesforce designed its reporting to serve the needs of its buyer, the sales team. The rest of Twilio's team was left wanting.

Step 3: Access Raw Data

Left without an alternative, the Twilio data team began uploading raw data to Amazon Web Services as either text files or basic databases. Employees could access the text files and process it themselves using a scripting language like Python or R. Alternatively, they could write their own SQL to query the data warehouse the data team configured.

Still, the majority of the company thirsted for data. Without the necessary coding skills, they were back at Step 1, asking favors from the engineers.

The Crux of the Problem

At each step of Twilio's data progression, the business faced the same problem. Two data-seeking constituencies existed within Twilio: the data team who could speak SQL and everyone else who couldn't.

Adept at navigating the full complexity of the data infrastructure, the data team values technical tools that expose the intricacy and the depth of the data latticework. In particular, the data team prizes software that transforms analyses from single efforts into productionized, automated reports that they could write once, but that would continue to run every day or every week and be sent to the right person in the business. These reusable analysis components meaningfully reduced the data team's workload, minimizing the length of the data breadline.

In contrast, the rest of the company values simple user interfaces that provide quick access to the subset of data relevant to a particular user and present the data in a clear, attractive visualization, ready to be pasted into a presentation or press release.

Unlike data teams who productionize data pipelines, business users explore data. In many cases, once a user has found an answer to a specific question, the project is finished and the analytical work on the project is unlikely to be used again.

Resolving that difference is the crux of the problem.

Bring Your Own BI: The Five Letters That Will Change the Data World

Products that enable scale, efficiency, and reusability don't often offer speed, ease of use, and appealing visuals. In the past, the data team, as part of the chief information officer's or chief technology officer's team, owned the purchasing decision for the business intelligence and data analysis tools for the company. Not surprisingly, these teams often choose the software that prioritizes their needs: scale, reproducibility, and efficiency. After all, the volume of inbound data requests is only going in one direction: up and to the right.

But that purchasing authority has been decentralized. It now resides amongst individual team leaders and departments. In 2014, the Corporate Executive Board studied the extent of this decentralization. That year, business users spent 30 percent of total software spend.[1]

This phenomenon is called Shadow IT because these purchasing decisions fall outside the purview of the traditional IT teams' procurement processes and control. Many software vendors have seized this opportunity. Shadow IT spend is now evenly distributed across marketing, sales, engineering, human resources, and finance software—all easily purchased with a credit card.

Each of these software vendors is rushing to provide its buyer with a customized and dedicated business intelligence tool. This movement is called BYOBI, for "bring your own business intelligence," a natural response to the problematic data supply chain that has historically failed to serve the needs of the business user, just as the Twilio example showed.

Figure 6.1 shows the way business intelligence software used to work. On the left-hand side, data engineers transform data from a handful of databases kept on the premises into an internal data warehouse. Then, the data is modeled and optimized for answering the questions the business has today. Reports and visualizations are configured for access in the future. Inevitably, those questions will evolve and new ones will arise. But at design time, those questions

---

[1]"Harnessing Business Led IT," November 6, 2015. Retrieved from www .executiveboard.com/exbd-resources/pdf/executive-guidance/eg2014-q2-final.pdf.

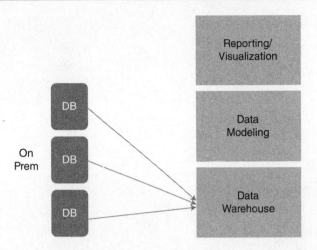

Figure 6.1 The Traditional On-Premise Business Intelligence Stack

are impossible to anticipate when the system is deployed for the first time. Inevitably, the BI tool fails to live up to its potential and teams can't access the data they need.

What's worse, with the explosion of cloud and software-as-a-service (SaaS) software use, the data-fragmentation problem has exploded. Today, company data isn't stored across a collection of databases within the company's firewalls but is scattered across thousands of servers all over the world as companies adopt SaaS products that store data in the cloud. It is a diaspora of data.

Nevertheless, teams still need to access, process, and analyze data, irrespective of where it resides. Faced with this problem, data teams must transform their data architecture into BYOBI.

Figure 6.2 illustrates BYOBI architecture.

There are four fundamental changes with BYOBI:

1. End users decide which reporting/visualization tools to use.
2. The IT and data teams' roles shift to creating and maintaining the support infrastructure to enable business users to analyze their data with BYOBI tools.
3. Cloud/SaaS databases become a key data contributor, complementing the on-premises databases, those controlled by the company.

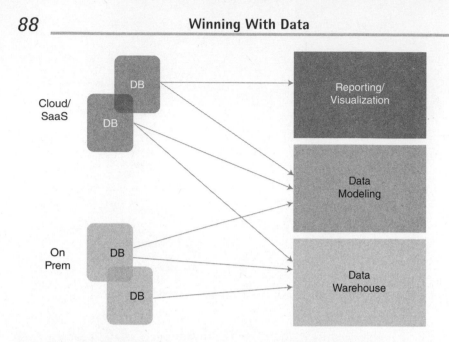

FIGURE 6.2   The Bring Your Own Business Intelligence (BYOBI) Stack

4. Reporting and visualization occur primarily on raw data, not a subset of data that has been transformed or optimized a priori.

BYOBI shifts the power to the end user rather than the data team. Of course, the end user favors ease of use, speed, and visual appeal and can finally procure it. With a solution just a credit card swipe away, many business teams procure their own business intelligence solutions.

Consequently, the company can end up with a large number of disparate data analysis tools, none of which work together. This fragmentation of analysis across teams and tools challenges the data team to ensure everyone within the company performs analysis consistently, using the same terminology and metrics. Unfettered like the Tower of Babylon, BYOBI will manifest a myriad of data silos and lead to a confusion of tongues: Different teams within the company will speak different languages.

Fortunately, data modeling combats this metrics fragmentation. Within every business, there is a handful of people who understand how all the data interleaves. Imagine if everyone within the business could manipulate data as if they understood how data interrelates, the way the data team does. Data modeling enables precisely this.

A data engineer describes once how to analyze data, and then a marketing team can aggregate purchasing data and marketing campaign data with just a few clicks, without having to consult the data team. If the marketing research project is a fact-finding expedition, then the report can be jettisoned when it is completed. Otherwise, the marketer can create an ongoing dashboard published on a web page or delivered by e-mail each week.

Data modeling empowers business users to create their own BI tools, supporting the BYOBI movement. At the same time, this technology supports the data team with a technical solution that enables efficient support of people across the company. A data team need specify the relationship between sales and marketing data only once. Then, everyone in the company benefits from this work.

For companies to succeed in deploying BYOBI infrastructure, they must find solutions that satisfy the needs of both constituencies in the company: those who enable access to the data and those who consume the data. Though they have divergent requirements in their experiences, with data modeling, it's possible to deploy one solution that satisfies both groups' needs.

The Power of a Unified Data-Modeling Layer

Not far from the Bronx Zoo, Wings Academy is a small public high school that educates about 500 students each year. In 1999, after having graduated from Yale with a degree in education and history, Charles Best began teaching high school social studies at Wings. Soon, he found his classroom budget limited, so he began spending his own money on school supplies.

After chatting about the limitations with many of his colleagues at Wings, Best hatched the idea for DonorsChoose.org, a nonprofit that allows anyone to donate to individual classroom projects. He wrote the first version of the website and told his colleagues at Wings about it.

Best's coworkers posted 10 different projects on the first version of the website. Best didn't know many donors, so he anonymously funded these first projects himself.

Amazed by their success, these 10 teachers spread the word that DonorsChoose.org worked. Three years later, Oprah Winfrey mentioned DonorsChoose.org on her television show. Viewers donated $250,000 to all kinds of classroom projects. Since then, DonorsChoose .org has captured the imaginations of people like comedian Stephen Colbert and Jeff Weiner, the CEO of LinkedIn, both of whom serve on the board. In addition, the charity counts many corporate sponsors, including Google, Chevron, Staples, Price Waterhouse Coopers, AT&T, and Disney.

As of 2015, DonorsChoose.org has funded more than 660,000 projects benefiting more than 17 million students across 66,000 schools. Two million people have donated $385 million to fund museum field trips, biology kits, school plays, and tablets in the classroom. Sixty percent of all the public schools in America have posted a project on DonorsChoose.org, and on average, their projects are financed within 27 days. After students receive their materials, they often send letters written in crayons or colored pencil to donors thanking them for their contributions.

Vladimir Dubovsky is a data scientist at DonorsChoose.org. He and his team have built a modern data fabric using Looker for DonorsChoose.org. With it, the data team has been able to serve internal and external constituencies.

Fundraising success is one of the greatest areas of data analysis for DonorsChoose.org. Donor appreciation managers at DonorsChoose.org seek to reward donors with gestures like handwritten thank-you notes from classrooms receiving funding. The team believed these notes would be effective ways to increase future donations from sponsors. But they didn't know quite how impactful a crayon drawing could be.

So, one donor appreciation manager analyzed the effect of handwritten notes on donor lifetime value and discovered a 50 percent increase. This meaningful boost spurred the nonprofit to redouble its efforts to send handwritten notes.

In addition to understanding its contributor base, DonorsChoose .org also studies teachers. On average, each teacher who fundraises on the platform attracts two new donors through his relationships. But the average hides some stellar outliers. More than 5,000 teachers have recruited 10 donors each, markedly improving the charity's ability to finance future projects.

DonorsChoose.org centralizes the teacher fundraising data to help the nonprofit understand its teacher base better, provide teachers with the right tools to improve their donor-recruiting ability, and identify teachers to support the charity's awareness campaigns.

In addition to all the support from teachers, large corporations donate substantially. DonorsChoose.org reports the impact of participation to its partners, including Best Buy and Amazon.

These are key relationships. DonorsChoose.org relies on Best Buy and Amazon to fulfill the requests of the teachers. For example, a teacher creates a fundraising proposal on DonorsChoose.org containing items from the DonorsChoose.org store hosted on Amazon. When a donor or a group of donors funds a project, the money is paid immediately to the retail partner, who ships the products to the classroom in a day or two.

Retail partners want to understand the impact and breadth of their participation in the DonorsChoose.org program, so the nonprofit provides these partners a login and a place to explore their data. Each partner logs into its dashboard to understand the inventory demand, inventory shipped by day, the top geographies requesting materials, and even the impact based on household income.

More recently, Staples and Google have partnered with DonorsChoose.org to perform flash fundings, where these two companies finance all the outstanding projects in a city. Staples has participated in eight campaigns, supporting 960 projects, which reach more than 90,000 students across Portland, Washington, DC, Chicago, and Philadelphia, among others.

These projects have a dual purpose: They broaden the public awareness of DonorsChoose.org and its cause. In addition, they create a halo effect around the corporate sponsors who finance education projects around the United States. The data DonorsChoose .org provides to these sponsors helps validate and justify their ongoing participation in these programs.

With data from nearly a decade of operations, DonorsChoose .org can predict its expected number of projects by time of year and provide an accurate forecast of the cash requirements. The

DonorsChoose.org data team uses this data to develop predictive models. Vlad Dubovsky, data scientist at DonorsChoose.org, explains:

> We have these flash funded campaigns, where we have a big funder say, "Look, I'm going to fund all schools in Fargo, North Dakota, or Chicago, on this day." They want to fund it in the future, obviously. If their question is, "What is it going to cost to fund all projects in December of 2016?" Then we have to run some analyses for the past few years, to track the differences, how the growth changed, and remove any seasonality, or anomalies, and all that.
>
> We actually use Looker for all of that. This is historical data analytics meets predictive data science, in one place. Our CEO is the biggest geek around these inventory dashboards. He loves them.[2]

DonorsChoose.org has adopted a platform that serves the needs of both its internal and external constituents. Data empowers teachers to recruit donors more effectively. Data informs the efforts of the donor appreciation managers. Data enables critical partnerships with large corporations that support the charity and improve the education of millions of American students.

That's the power of a single tool that satisfies both the sophisticated needs of the data team and the simpler needs of the marketing, donation management, and public relations teams.

The Final Step: A Data Fabric

Finally, Twilio, like DonorsChoose.org, adopted Looker. Looker empowers the data team to describe the data structure within an organization once and for all. This abstraction layer, a data fabric, allows anyone within the company to step to the plate and analyze the data with all the knowledge of the data team.

Jessica, a performance marketing lead at Twilio, who optimizes paid acquisition spend and search engine optimization for the company, relies on the shared data fabric to intelligently deploy marketing spend in a way that's consistent with the rest of the organization.

---

[2]Vlad Dubovskiy, "Centralizing Data at DonorsChoose," YouTube, April 7, 2015. Retrieved from https://www.youtube.com/watch?v=2OAsKqKapX4.

She explains, "I'm on a very cross functional team, so sometimes I need to borrow concepts from other teams like finance to understand how they calculate ROI [return-on-investment] so that I can apply that to my recommendations and feedback, and so that they are consistent internally."[3]

The shared data fabric and universal data dictionary give Jessica confidence. She can be certain that when she analyzes her marketing campaigns' return on investment, she is using the definition created by the finance team for the entire company. When she presents her recommendations to her VP of marketing or decides on her own to prioritize one campaign over another, Jessica knows the ROI figures are consistent and accurate, and that she'll make the right decision.

Collaboration of this scale is rare among large companies, particularly those with greater than a few hundred employees. In most businesses, data silos inhibit the adoption of universal metrics. In a siloed world, Jessica's marketing efforts would not be nearly as effective as they are today.

Not limited to one department, the benefits of this data fabric extend to the Twilio carrier management teams. One of Twilio's products enables developers to purchase or rent telephone numbers via a simple API call, a message from one computer to Twilio's servers sent over the Internet. Twilio maintains an inventory of phone numbers in every country and area code demanded by its customers. As Twilio sells phone numbers in one geography, it must restock the inventory by purchasing new numbers from telephone carriers.

An analyst at Twilio described one of the key issues faced by the telephone number inventory team:

> Our phone number inventory at Twilio is a huge data problem in itself.... We have to keep track of the different aspects of [these phone numbers].... And it's incredibly multidimensional problem.... Some of [these phone numbers] can send SMS, some of them can send MMS. Being able to access that data set in a flexible way is incredibly important to us making sure that we have the right phone numbers in stock.[4]

---

[3] "How the Right BI Can Fundamentally Change Your Organization," Vimeo, July 2015. Retrieved from https://vimeo.com/132107783.
[4] Ibid.

This data dictates the efforts of Twilio's procurement team and influences the marketing campaigns of Jessica's team. The procurement team must acquire the right assortment of telephone numbers with different functionality. And the marketing team must generate the demand to sell those phone numbers profitably.

Only by unifying the data and creating a centralized view that each team member can use for his own purposes can Twilio achieve this kind of efficiency and collaboration across the company.

Twilio's progression through the four different phases of data architecture for modern companies is representative of the journey of many cutting-edge businesses. At each point in the process, an iterative solution solves a hair-on-fire problem but also creates more bottlenecks.

At Twilio's outset, data requests consumed the time of engineers, who had to respond to all the incoming requests from across the company, in addition to building the core product.

Next, the data engineering team struggled to shoehorn the company's data in Salesforce. A sales-focused solution, this workaround failed to meet the needs of the rest of the company.

Then, Twilio's data team provided access to raw databases and text files to the employee base. Unfortunately, only a handful of the team could write the necessary code and scripts to generate the data they needed themselves.

Finally, Twilio deployed new data-modeling technology that enabled the data team to serve all the different departments in a company and allow employees to explore data as they need it.

The fundamental technology innovation here is the data fabric. Data scientists and engineers understand the structure and organization of data within most companies, but most everyone else is in the dark. For everyone else to manipulate the data as if they were data analysts, a company must architect a common data fabric.

Chapter 7

Data Literacy and Empowerment: The Core Responsibilities of the Data Team

The Illusion of Validity: How to Avoid Data Biases

When you develop your opinions on the basis of weak evidence, you will have difficulty interpreting subsequent information that contradicts these opinions, even if this new information is obviously more accurate.

—Nassim Nicholas Taleb

They operated from a clandestine apartment in Harlem, a block from Columbia University, at 401 West 118th Street. A cell comprising 18 of the most respected American mathematicians and statisticians spirited data sets up the stairs, analyzed them, and stole to Washington, DC, on military aircraft to present the results of their ruminations to the admirals of the navy and the marines and the generals of the army, marines, and air force during the Second World War.[1] Allen Wallis, director of the Statistical Research Group (SRG), said of his team, "This was surely the most extraordinary group of statisticians ever organized." He continued:

"Perhaps the strongest encouragement was the fact that when we made recommendations, frequently things happened. Fighter planes entered combat with their machine guns loaded according to Jack

---

[1] M. Friedman and R. D. Friedman, *Two Lucky People: Memoirs* (Chicago: University of Chicago Press, 1998), 181.

Wolfowitz's recommendations about mixing types of ammunition, and maybe the pilots came back or maybe they didn't. Navy planes launched rockets whose propellants had been accepted by Gabe Girshick's sampling-inspection plans, and maybe the rockets exploded and destroyed our own planes and pilots or maybe they destroyed the target. During the Battle of the Bulge in December 1944, several high-ranking army officers flew to Washington from the battle, spent the day discussing the best settings on proximity fuses for air bursts of artillery shells against ground troops and flew back to the battle so they could put into effect advice from, among others, Milton Friedman whose earlier studies of the fuses had given him extensive and accurate knowledge of the way the fuses actually performed."[2]

Many of these men relocated their families abruptly to Manhattan, called to serve their country. Chief among them was Abraham Wald, a Rumanian prodigy. A Jew, Wald respected the Sabbath on Saturday and wasn't permitted to attend Rumanian school on Saturdays. His erudite parents homeschooled him, and Abraham graduated with a doctorate in mathematics from the University of Vienna in 1931. In 1938, he fled Nazism in Austria for New York. He began to teach statistics at Columbia University.

Soon thereafter, the SRG recruited Wald to join them. The U.S. Air Force needed desperately to solve a key problem. Allied planes in the European and Pacific theaters were being shot down at an astonishing rate. During the course of the war, more than 43,581 planes would be lost to flak cannons, the Luftwaffe, and Japanese Zeros.[3] In a single 376-plane raid in August 1943, 60 B-17s were shot down. The loss rates were so great that it was statistically impossible for a serviceman to survive a 25-mission tour of duty in Europe.

With airmen facing impossible odds, the SRG tasked Wald to design and develop a new armor layout for aircraft flying in enemy territory. The air force wanted to reinforce planes but could add armor only to a small section of the plane. Each pound of armor reduced

[2]M. Friedman and R. D. Friedman, *Two Lucky People: Memoirs* (Chicago: University of Chicago Press, 1998), 132.

[3]"WWII Aircraft Facts," World War II Foundation, 2014. Retrieved from www.wwiifoundation.org/students/wwii-aircraft-facts/.

the bomb payload capacity by one pound, diminishing the attack capability of the fleet.

To inform the analysis, the air force supplied Wald with data from the front. Servicemen recorded the number and placement of bullet holes on the fuselage, wings, and tails of all the planes that returned to base. Returning bombers bore scars concentrated around the tail gunner and the wings. So, the leaders of the air force suggested reinforcing these bullet-riddled regions with armor.

Wald vehemently disagreed.

The returning planes' pockmarks showed where the birds were strongest, the places they could suffer injury yet still return to base. The fuselage and wings least needed the armor to survive. These planes suffered injuries in these regions and returned to base regardless. Wald argued this proved these areas weren't critical.

There were tens of thousands of planes that hadn't returned home because they'd been struck elsewhere: the engines, the tail, and the cockpit.[4] Those areas should be armored more heavily.

The oversight by the U.S. Air Force, dubbed "survivorship bias," is a cognitive bias that plagues data analysts in all fields. In 1987, a group of researchers studied the survival rates of cats falling from buildings. They observed cats that fell from six stories or fewer suffer greater injuries than those that fall from above six stories.[5]

They offered a theory that cats reach terminal velocity after having fallen more than 6 stories. No longer accelerating toward the ground, the cats relaxed. When they finally landed, the relaxed cats' more supple muscles absorbed the impact of the fall.

The issue with the study, of course, is survivorship. The hospital that gathered the data only examined cats that had been brought into the clinic. Felines falling from six stories or fewer are brought to the veterinarian much more frequently than those that fall from greater heights, who unfortunately, didn't survive. The researchers didn't consider the fatalities in their analysis, skewing the data and reaching a specious conclusion.

---

[4]M. Mangel and F. J. Samaniego, "Abraham Wald's Work on Aircraft Survivability: Rejoinder." *Journal of the American Statistical Association* 79, no. 386 (1984): 270.
[5]W. O. Whitney and C. J. Mehlhaff, "High-Rise Syndrome in Cats," *Journal of the American Veterinary Medical Association 191*, no. 11 (1987): 1399–1403.

Survivorship bias also occurs frequently in financial analysis. Mutual and hedge funds that produce poor returns compared to their peers frequently merge with more successful groups. When analysts perform long-term studies of these funds' performance, the underperforming funds are no longer part of the data set, boosting overall returns. In his paper "Returns from Investing in Equity Mutual Funds 1971–1991," Burton Malkiel, a Princeton economist and former director of the Vanguard Group, demonstrated overall mutual performance is distorted by 1.5 percentage points, boosting reported returns by more than 20 percent.

Survivorship bias materializes when we omit certain data from our analysis. The remaining data, containing the survivors, leads us to draw a faulty conclusion. When analyzing data, it's critical to ensure the analysis evaluates the entirety of the relevant population, not just those who have survived.

Correlation versus Causation

In addition to survivorship bias, many other problems plague analyses. Confusing correlation and causation is another bias.

Tyler Vigen, a Harvard graduate student, has written a book called *Spurious Correlations* to prove the point. Vigen wrote a computer program to identify highly correlated data sets and produce charts for his website.

While the number of Americans who drown in pools may correlate at 66 percent with the number of films in which Nicolas Cage stars, Cage doesn't cause those accidents. Nor do margarine makers influence divorce rates in Maine, regardless of the 99 percent correlation between those two trends. These numbers just happen to move in tandem.

Anchoring Bias

If I were to ask you if Gandhi was more than 114 years old when he died, your estimate of his age at his death would be much higher than if I changed the age to 35. This is called an anchoring bias and is well documented by Nobel laureate Daniel Kahneman in his book *Thinking, Fast and Slow*. Anchoring bias occurs when you are asked to consider a value before estimating.

AVAILABILITY BIAS

The 2016 Powerball began as a jackpot of $40 million. Powerballs were drawn 19 times without a lottery player having chosen the right combination of the six numbers. Without a winner, the lottery rolls the previous jackpot into the next drawing. The mammoth and growing jackpot attracted press, which in turn generated more demand for tickets.

Forty-four U.S. states and two territories sold tickets and pooled the proceeds together to amass the second-largest jackpot in history. All told, the final Powerball jackpot totaled $1.6 billion. Mathematicians projected a 1 in 292 million chance of winning Powerball. Only Spain's El Gordo lottery, meaning the "Fat One," raised more, at $2.4 billion.

When someone does leap from his couch with a winning ticket, lotteries like the Powerball and El Gordo rush to the stores that sold the winning tickets and televise ecstatic newly minted multimillionaires, in part because it's fun, but also to stoke the availability bias.

If we can remember an event more easily, we believe it to be more probable. The Powerball's motto underscores this point: "Hey, you never know."

Availability biases also exist in the workplace. After hearing about a particularly dissatisfied customer, a management team may believe the prevalence of unhappy buyers to be much greater than the reality.

ILLUSION OF VALIDITY

Last, the illusion of validity fools us into believing that gathering more data will help us predict the future better. Nobel laureate Daniel Kahneman also coined this term.

Kahneman and a colleague devised a test called the leaderless group challenge. Eight soldiers were gathered on a field and dressed in plain clothes to hide their rank and seniority from each other and from Kahneman. These eight men were ordered to lift and carry a piece of timber from one side of a field to another, over a six-foot wall. If the log touched the ground or the wall, the eight men were to start over again.

Kahneman described his observations:

> As a colleague and I monitored the exercise, we made note of who took charge, who tried to lead but was rebuffed, how much each soldier contributed to the group effort. We saw who seemed to be

stubborn, submissive, arrogant, patient, hot-tempered, persistent or a quitter. We sometimes saw competitive spite when someone whose idea had been rejected by the group no longer worked very hard. And we saw reactions to crisis: who berated a comrade whose mistake caused the whole group to fail, who stepped forward to lead when the exhausted team had to start over. Under the stress of the event, we felt, each man's true nature revealed itself in sharp relief.

After watching the candidates go through several such tests, we had to summarize our impressions of the soldiers' leadership abilities with a grade and determine who would be eligible for officer training.... Because our impressions of how well each soldier performed were generally coherent and clear, our formal predictions were just as definite. We rarely experienced doubt or conflicting impressions.[6]

Then Kahneman compared the progress of the cadets in their military careers to his estimations. Despite the resolute confidence in his assessment of each cadet's future success from his observations of the log experiment, Kahneman's forecasts were largely useless. They failed to predict those who would become officers better than a coin flip would.

He named this bias the illusion of validity: Passion, conviction, enthusiasm, and resolve might make us feel more confident in our decision, but they don't improve the probability we've made the correct choice.

There are many types of cognitive bias. The first step in data literacy is avoiding these types of bias by becoming aware of them.

How Facebook and Zendesk Engender Data Literacy

The greatest value of a picture is when it forces us to notice what we never expected to see.

　　　　　　　　　　　　　　　　　　　　　—John Tukey

Analyzing data without care for these types of data bias can lead to fallacious conclusions. To ensure employees across the

---

[6]B. G. Malkiel, "Returns from Investing in Equity Mutual Funds 1971 to 1991," *The Journal of Finance* 50, no. 2 (1995): 549–572.

business mind these challenges, all new employees at Facebook attend a two-week data camp run by the Facebook data team.[7]

Every analyst at Facebook is required to attend, but others are invited; product managers, designers, finance analysts, engineers, and operations teams also join. These camps cultivate data literacy within the company. This data literacy provides Facebook employees a common language of data with which to discuss and analyze problems.

In the mornings, instructors educate the class about the available tools and data sets within Facebook. There are more than 10,000 database tables within the company—more than one per employee.

In the afternoon, employees work on self-selected projects, often real issues the company is facing. According to former leader of the team Ken Rudin, "We have a running collection of problems that business units are working on, and we ask the Data Camp participants, analysts, project managers, designers, engineers, people from finance, to think through the problem."[8]

Throughout the program, the Facebook data team aims to teach people the right mind-set: how to develop hypotheses, how to frame them so they can be answered by data, and how to test them. When a data team trains its colleagues in data literacy, the team becomes a huge lever for the business and a powerful tool for eliminating data breadlines.

"We really want everyone to feel like they are capable of using data. Then analysts aren't a bottleneck to getting things done. They're there for doing the SWAT team types of things that take a little extra scale and more depth than your average person would have," said Rudin.[9]

This notion of data literacy isn't unique to Facebook. AvantCredit, one of the fastest-growing lending institutions in the United States,

---

[7]M. Lev-Ram, "What I Learned at Facebook's Big Data Bootcamp," *Fortune*, June 13, 2013. Retrieved from http://fortune.com/2013/06/13/what-i-learned-at-facebooks-big-data-bootcamp/.

[8]D. Henschen, "5 Lessons from Facebook on Analytics Success," *Information-Week*, November 20, 2013. Retrieved from www.informationweek.com/software/information-management/5-lessons-from-facebook-on-analytics-success/d/d-id/898903.

[9]M. Lev-Ram, "What I Learned at Facebook's Big Data Bootcamp," *Fortune*, June 13, 2013. Retrieved from http://fortune.com/2013/06/13/what-i-learned-at-facebooks-big-data-bootcamp/.

requires all of its employees to attend a two-week seminar on the data infrastructure and data tools the company uses. The data team members at Kickstarter, the popular crowd-funding site, embed themselves within teams inside the company to teach data skills in informal sessions. In addition, they hold regular reading groups and office hours. Last, the data team publishes a biweekly newsletter containing all the key data for the company in the past 14 days.

Zendesk's data team, which numbers 30 people in a company of about 1,000, has also adopted a teaching philosophy. Once per week, the team hosts office hours. Product managers, product marketing managers, sales people, PR teammates, and engineers pop in and, according to the director of data Jason Maynard, always start the conversation the same way: "I have this question…"

One member of the Zendesk data team pairs with the questioner and spends the next 30 to 45 minutes working through the issue. First, they find the relevant data set together. Next, they process the data in the best tool together. Last, they reach the answer. Then, it's on to the next one.

In addition to these office hours, the data team hosts monthly Data Days in each of the company's four offices: San Francisco, Singapore, Montpelier (France), and Melbourne. These Data Days resemble Facebook's data boot camp to some extent. In the first week of training, the Zendesk team covers the basic principles of data literacy:

◆ **SQL:** Also known as structured query language; the most basic language for asking questions of data tools
◆ **Data architecture:** Where to find all the different data sets that employees might care to query
◆ **Data dictionary:** A review of the key metrics and their definitions that are used across the company
◆ **Case studies:** Accounts of previous problems product and marketing teams have faced within the company, and a step-by-step recreation of how those teams solved the problems
◆ **Basic statistical concepts:** Sample size considerations, estimation, sample bias, confidence intervals, and significance

- ◆ **Storytelling with data:** How to construct an argument with data and visualizations
- ◆ **Actionability:** Determining whether this data analysis will result in a tangible change in the way the company operates

In addition to formulating hypotheses and designing experiments that can be invalidated or validated by data, data literacy also means converting these insights into impact. The goal of all these analyses isn't just to report what is happening or what the team observed. Nor is it simply to identify the actionable insights that could be taken. Rather, it's impact—improving the team's plan or a key metric in a meaningful way.

As word of Zendesk spread across the globe, customers asked the company to localize the software. In addition to the predominant English version, Zendesk has been translated into more than 25 other languages, including German, Italian, Russian, Thai, Finnish, and Chinese.

More than just changing the text of the software, localization requires billing in the local currency of the Zendesk customer, creating marketing landing pages in the native language, and hiring salespeople and marketers who speak that language to generate more business.

At Zendesk, like many other companies, localization occurs piecemeal. First, localized landing pages are created. Then, the product is translated. Last, Zendesk hires a team of fluent speakers in the language. Each step costs time, effort, and money.

The Zendesk product team wondered how each of these three steps impacted a customer's proclivity to convert from a trial to a paid user. So, they created a conversion funnel to measure the impact, step by step, of customers in different regions and contrasted the conversion rates of those with just a product translated and those with the full localization completed. They found conversion rates doubled compared to a partial localization effort. The data more than justified fully localizing the software in key customer geographics.

All of these companies' data teams supporting the company have adopted a mission to shepherd a company's employees through four key processes: developing the right metrics and language, educating teams to analyze data without bias, rewarding curiosity with the best tools to find the right information, and maximizing the speed of the company to decide.

Data education, data literacy, and data tooling are three key ingredients to evolving a company's culture to becoming more data-driven.

Walking the Data Gemba: Training by Walking Around

In Japanese, *gemba* means "the real place." Japanese detectives refer to the crime scene as the *gemba*. Far-flung Japanese news correspondents report from the *gemba*. And the managers of the Toyota production line walk the *gemba*—the factory floor—the place where things are really happening.

The history of *gemba* starts more than 150 years ago. Sakichi Toyoda was born in 1867 into a family of farmers and carpenters. Eschewing the family businesses, he traveled from Yamaguchi, his hometown, to Tokyo, where he became fascinated with motors and machines. He resolved to bring this technology home. Soon after, he developed the first motorized loom to weave fabric and incorporated Toyoda Boshuku to commercialize the invention.

As Toyoda refined these looms, he identified thread quality as a limiting factor to efficiency. Unreliable thread broke, stopping the production of the machines and leaving early technicians to wonder whether the thread broke because it was shoddy or because a snag in the loom had snapped it. To solve this problem, Toyoda built a spinning plant to manufacture high-quality thread to maximize the efficiency of his looms.

A relentless tinkerer, Toyoda incubated a car company within the loom business. He spun out Toyota Motor, a car maker, in 1934. But, the separation would not last long. During World War II, the Japanese government consolidated industrial companies and fused the Toyoda Automatic Loom and Toyota Motor. Eventually, this combined entity would become the modern-day $200 billion market cap industrial behemoth Toyota.[10]

---

[10]"The History of Toyoda Boshoku," Toyota Boshoku Corporation, January 2008. Retrieved from www.toyota-boshoku.com/global/special/discover/history01/index.html.

As the demand for Toyoda's cars increased, he sought to improve the efficiency of his manufacturing lines. Toyota pioneered a manufacturing philosophy called the Toyota Production System (TPS), which maximizes manufacturing efficiency. Two of Toyoda's lieutenants, Taiichi Ohno and Eiji Toyoda, developed TPS over the course of 25 years, creating and refining concepts like just-in-time inventory, a scheduling system called *kanban*, and *jidoka*, a mechanism for handing anomalies on the production line.[11]

In addition, they developed the Gemba Walk. Floor managers walked the *gemba*—the place where work is being done—to build relationships with employees, identify problem areas in the manufacturing flow, chart and record key metrics of the production line, and understand if the workers had the supplies they needed.

The *gemba* idea crossed the Pacific when the executive team at Hewlett-Packard colloquialized the idea into "management by wandering around" (MBWA) in the 1970s and 1980s.[12] MBWA asked managers to randomly stop and ask HP workers how things at the company were progressing. The serendipity of chance encounters with many employees provided executives at HP a deeper understanding of the state of their business—what was working and what wasn't.

At Facebook, analysts walk the *gemba*. Years ago, Facebook wrestled with the question of how to structure its data team to maximize their impact. A centralized data team structure, where analysts sit together and report to a common head of the team, ensures the team unifies their processes and analyses, to maintain consistency and maximize efficiency. But separated teams become more reactive than embedded data analysts, awaiting requests from other areas of the business rather than seizing the initiative.

Facebook also considered decentralizing the analysts. In this scenario, the analysts would sit with their product teams and report to the product leader. The decentralized approach ensured analyst proactivity—the analysts would attend many of the product team meetings and could respond instantly to needs—but this

---

[11]Toyota Production System, n.d. Retrieved January 30, 2016, from https://en.wikipedia.org/wiki/Toyota_Production_System.

[12]"Management by Walking About," *The Economist*, September 8, 2008. Retrieved www.economist.com/node/12075015.

decentralized structure created a new set of problems. In particular, the data analysts would duplicate many of the same analyses as their peers working with other teams in the company. This redundancy would reduce the efficiency of the team and create data silos, with different teams reporting different numbers for the same metrics, inciting data brawls.

To get the best of both worlds, Facebook ultimately elected a hybrid approach it calls the embedded model. Analysts report to the head of analysis at Facebook as in a centralized model, but they sit with their teams as in a decentralized model to be proactive. This architecture ensures the company develops universal data analysis processes and maximizes the proactivity of the data analysts. Active participants in the daily meetings of the team, the analysts amass greater context for their work and broaden their impact to the teams. In this organizational design, the data analysts adopt the goals of their teams. This is how they walk the *gemba*.

Embedded within the respective product teams, data analysts at Facebook and other companies frequently come across critical problems that require escalation. For example, a product team may have just released the first version of a new product. The entire data supply chain to analyze this product must be created. Such a task is often beyond the means of the typical business analyst and requires collaboration across potentially several different teams, including the product team, the data analyst team, and perhaps the data infrastructure team.

When critical problems stop the Toyota automobile manufacturing lines, managers convene a *jishuken*. *Jishukens* are a series of meetings across functions to remedy an unexpected problem that must be escalated to managers. They have two goals: a learning goal and a productivity goal.

During the learning phase, the cross-functional team asks questions to understand the source of the issue. In our hypothetical product case, typical questions might include these: How much data do we need to collect? Which data do we need to collect? How will the data be analyzed? Who should the data be delivered to? How frequently must this data be collected?

By asking a series of questions, the team can understand the needs of the project. The team leader documents all of these questions and ensures that a proposed solution meets the needs of all the different stakeholders. This concludes the learning goal.

Next, the team implements the proposed solution, educates the remainder of the teams, and measures the performance of the solution over time to ensure that the solution they've designed satisfies the design requirements discovered in the learning phase.

At the conclusion of a *jishuken*, the team should have understood the problem, designed a workaround, and educated the relevant teams about the problem's origin and solution.

By walking the *gemba* the way Facebook data teams embed themselves within business functions, and by escalating new data challenges in *jishukens*, companies can ensure consistent, reliable, and accurate data pipelines. Like Toyoda's automobile manufacturing lines, data pipelines can benefit from lean management principles.

Chapter 8

Deeper Analyses: Asking the Right Questions

The formulation of a problem is often more essential than its solution, which may be merely a matter of mathematical or experimental skill. To raise new questions, new possibilities, to regard old problems from a new angle, requires creative imagination and marks real advances.

—Albert Einstein

After a company has evolved through the four steps of basic data architecture, the way Twilio has, they begin to ask, "What's next?" Gartner, the market research agency, created the Data Sophistication Journey to answer the question.

The Data Sophistication Journey maps a team's progression from descriptive analytics to diagnostic analytics, and from predictive analytics to prescriptive analytics. Each step demands more of the team than the last but provides incremental value for the effort.

Descriptive analytics encapsulates the dashboards that dot corporate walls and fill e-mail inboxes. These reports convey how metrics have changed over time and provide teams visibility into their execution relative to plans and goals. See Figure 8.1.

Diagnostic analysis answers questions such as "Why did sales increase last quarter?" More than simply tabulating sums and generating growth rates, diagnostic analytics requires a deeper understanding of statistics. It correlates different factors to determine which relationships might be causal.

Did one region's sales team outperform? Did Japan's currency meaningfully appreciate relative to the dollar, boosting sales in Asia

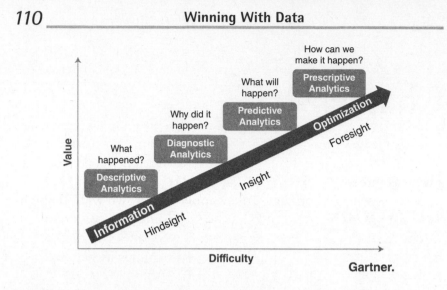

FIGURE 8.1 Gartner's Data Sophistication Journey

Pacific? Did the European team raise prices or run a promotion? Each of these facets must be considered and judged in an automated way using correlations to perform diagnostic analytics.

Predictive analytics uses historical data to project the future. Given our current sales pipeline and our historical prospect close rates and sales cycles, will our bookings number meet our target this year? Predictive analytics empowers companies to evaluate different scenarios, to answer the question "What if?" What if we were to hire two new field salespeople in the United States? Could we exceed our targets by 10 percent?

Prescriptive analytics, the zenith of Gartner's journey, suggest the right course of action given the data: Hire four new salespeople over the next three months to attain your plan. Very few companies have deployed prescriptive analytics because the volumes of data required and the sophistication of the data analysis are beyond the capabilities of most businesses.

The major advancement in these four-step processes occurs between diagnostic and predictive analytics. Descriptive and diagnostic analytics describe historical data. They elucidate the past. Predictive analytics forecast scenarios of what might happen in the future.

But Gartner's journey is missing an important step in between Steps 2 and 3: exploratory analytics. Unlike the descriptive statistics we use to understand the past, which seek to verify that a hypothesis explains why an event occurred, we can use exploratory analytics to search for hypotheses. This isn't a new concept. It dates back to the mid-twentieth century.

A native of Portland, Maine, John Tukey stunned his parents when he informed them that a bridge crossing the Susquehanna River was closed, and they should change their route. John had read a notice in the paper just that morning announcing the construction project. John was three.[1]

A homeschooled prodigy, Tukey applied to Brown with the highest SAT score recorded by the Educational Testing Service. After graduating from Brown with a degree in chemistry, he earned a PhD in mathematics from Princeton. With the United States in the throes of the Second World War, Tukey joined the Fire Control Research Office on 20 Nassau Street in Princeton. There he employed statistics to model the ballistic dynamics of rocket fuel and break the encryption of the Nazi Enigma machine.

In addition, he collaborated with the leading minds of the era. He worked with John von Neumann, the father of the atomic bomb, on early computer designs; influenced the computer industry by collaborating with Claude Shannon, the father of information theory; and "made more original contributions to statistics than anyone else since World War II."[2]

Most important for the world of data analysis, Tukey introduced a distinction between exploratory data analysis and confirmatory data analysis. Confirmatory data analysis is another name for the statistics we learn in our college Stats 101 course. Also called hypothesis testing, confirmatory data analysis seeks to prove that a particular idea is true with a reasonable amount of confidence.

In contrast, exploratory data analysis doesn't seek to prove or disprove a particular idea using data. Rather, it suggests hypotheses for patterns we're observing in our businesses. Data exploration starts with the question "Why?" Why are sales increasing in the East but declining in the West? Why does this customer segment purchase

---

[1]D. R. Brillinger, "John W. Tukey: His life and Professional Contributions," *The Annals of Statistics* 30, no. 6 (2002): 1535–1575.
[2]S. Schultz, "Statistician John W. Tukey Dies," press release, Princeton University, July 26, 2000. Retrieved from https://www.princeton.edu/pr/news/00/q3/0727-tukey.htm.

twice as frequently as another? Why does this marketing campaign generate positive return on investment in contrast to all the others?

Exploratory data analysis is far more common in businesses than confirmatory data analysis, because unexpected patterns and events pop up all the time. Our innate human curiosity spurs us to seek the causes for these observations so we can put them into context, understand what they mean, and learn from them.

More than 30 years ago, Tukey recognized data exploration required new tools, and his seminal book on the topic, *Exploratory Data Analysis*, published in 1977, started the movement to create data exploration tools. Since then, there has been a substantial lineage of statistical analysis tools including IBM S-Plus, SAS, R, and Mathematical, among others.

But, these tools have remained esoteric curiosities for most workers in America. Hundreds of millions of people use Microsoft Excel, the most basic data-exploration tool. But only a few hundred thousand to a few million employ more sophisticated statistical packages.

In the past five years, database and data-exploration technologies have become powerful enough, inexpensive enough, and approachable enough for the millions of Microsoft users to explore their companies' data sets. Consequently, employees at every level of a company are now fully equipped to be able to explore their own data, develop hypotheses of their own, and answer questions they face in their daily work lives.

Exploratory analytics doesn't seek to answer the question "What happened?" Rather, it empowers people to see what is happening right now. This is the key to operationalizing data, to changing the way we operate our teams and our businesses in the afternoon because of data we see in the morning. Though it hasn't been recognized as a key step yet, it will be.

When Data Confounds Our Intuition: How to Handle Ambiguity

> *It is not what people do not know that's the problem. It is what they believe to be universal truths and refuse to reconsider that caused the difficulties.*
>
> —Martin Bruce

Suppose you've been selected to participate in a game show. The game show host asks you to pick one of three doors. Behind one, the grand prize awaits. Behind the other two are goats. You choose Door 1. Then the host opens Door 3, revealing a goat. The host prompts you again, "Would you like to select Door 2?" Should you choose it?

This statistics question rose to fame in 1990 when Marilyn Vos Savant asked it in *Parade* magazine. Vos Savant argued yes, you should.

In the weeks that followed, Vos Savant received more than 10,000 letters pronouncing her wrong. One thousands of these letters had been penned by PhDs, and many bore the insignia of prestigious universities.[3]

A professor of mathematics at Georgetown University wrote, "You are utterly incorrect. How many irate mathematicians are needed to get you to change your mind?" Another from George Mason University piled on, "You blew it! ... As a professional mathematician, I'm very concerned with the general public's lack of mathematical skills. Please help by confessing your error and, in the future, being more careful." Even Paul Erdos, the famed mathematician, refused to believe the result until it was proven to him by Monte Carlo simulation.

To the chagrin of the 10,000 vehement and highly educated contradictors, the result stands. Vindicated, Vos Savant exposed the often counterintuitive nature of probability.

There are many different ways to explain why selecting Door 2 will grant you a 67 percent chance of choosing the car. This is the simplest I've found. When you choose Door 1, you have a 33 percent chance of winning the car (1 in 3 doors). You also have a 2/3 chance that the car is not behind Door 1. After the host reveals Door 3 hides a goat, there is still a 2/3 chance that the car is not behind Door 1. But now there is only one door, Door 2. So you have a 2/3 chance that the car is behind Door 2. The additional information that Door 3 contains a goat improves your chances, and this can be proven using Bayes's Theorem.

But even after that explanation, the answer remains unintuitive.

[3]J. Tierney, "Behind Monty Hall's Doors: Puzzle, Debate and Answer?," *New York Times*, July 20, 1991. Retrieved from www.nytimes.com/1991/07/21/us/behind-monty-hall-s-doors-puzzle-debate-and-answer.html.

These confounding conclusions aren't rare. K. C. Cole, a professor at the University of Southern California, explained our challenge in perceiving the relative sizes of quantities in an article entitled "Why You Didn't See It Coming."

As Cole puts it, "Both $1 million and $1 billion sound like 'a lot,' … [But] even those who understand the true scale of the chasm between those numbers intellectually don't always 'get it' viscerally. It feels like the difference between a million and a billion is closer to a factor of three than a factor of 1,000. That's because our brain naturally works using something like a logarithmic scale, so that it can condense information like vast ranges in loudness and brightness efficiently. That can get us into trouble."[4]

> John Allen Paulos illustrates the often confounding nature of big numbers in his book *Innumeracy*: For example, knowing that it takes only about eleven and a half days for a million seconds to tick away, whereas almost thirty-two years are required for a billion seconds to pass, gives one a better grasp of the relative magnitudes of these two common numbers.[5]

These blindspots confuse us. And when prompted with data that confounds our expectations, only 10 percent of the time will we trust the data rather than our intuition, according to the *Economist* Intelligence Unit's "Decisive Actions: How Businesses Make Decisions" report. Fifty-seven percent of the time, we ask to reanalyze the data.[6]

Our ultimate goal with data is to mitigate those biases and reveal these fallacious cognitive facades. In the "Philosophy of Data," *New York Times* op-ed columnist David Brooks articulates the two ways data exposes when our hunches are just plain wrong.

> First, it's really good at exposing when our intuitive view of reality is wrong. For example, every person who plays basketball and nearly

---

[4]K. Cole, "Why You Didn't See It Coming," Scaling, *Nautilus* 29, October 15, 2015. Retrieved from http://nautil.us/issue/29/scaling/why-you-didnt-see-it-coming.

[5]J. A. Paulos, *Innumeracy: Mathematical Illiteracy and Its Consequences* (New York: Hill and Wang, 1988).

[6]*The Economist* Intelligence Unit, "Decisive Action: How Businesses Make Decisions and How They Could Do It Better," n.d. Retrieved January 29, 2016, from www.economistinsights.com/sites/default/files/Decisive Action - How businesses make decisions.pdf.

every person who watches it believes that players go through hot streaks, when they are in the groove, and cold streaks, when they are just not feeling it. But Thomas Gilovich, Amos Tversky and Robert Vallone found that a player who has made six consecutive foul shots has the same chance of making his seventh as if he had missed the previous six foul shots.

When a player has hit six shots in a row, we imagine that he has tapped into some elevated performance groove. In fact, it's just random statistical noise, like having a coin flip come up tails repeatedly. Each individual shot's success rate will still devolve back to the player's career shooting percentage....

Second, data can illuminate patterns of behavior we haven't yet noticed. For example, I've always assumed that people who frequently use words like "I," "me," and "mine" are probably more egotistical than people who don't. But as James Pennebaker of the University of Texas notes in his book, *The Secret Life of Pronouns*, when people are feeling confident, they are focused on the task at hand, not on themselves. High status, confident people use fewer "I" words, not more.[7]

Data is a powerful tool to expose our biases and point the way to the right decision, especially when the data contradicts our instincts. If 1,000 PhDs can be fooled by a counterintuitive probability problem, no one is safe from bias. So let's look at the data.

Data Is Useless Unless You Can Act On It

Not everything that counts can be counted. And not everything that can be counted, counts.

—Albert Einstein

Data for the sake of data, or analysis for its own sake, isn't valuable to anybody. What if I shared with you an analysis of the question "How many syllables do our salespeople speak when delivering client pitches and how has that changed over time?" The trend is certain to uncover some insights about marketing language, the disposition of the sales team, and how quickly they speak. But the question won't

---

[7]David Brooks, "The Philosophy of Data," *New York Times*, February 5, 2013.

lead to a change in the team's operations, no matter how in-depth the analysis.

Expensify, a 100-person San Francisco–based company, has developed a real-time expense report used by millions. At the conclusion of a sales dinner after the bill is paid (and the prospective customer is satisfied both with the meal and the terms of the contract!), a sales executive photographs the receipt, types the name of the prospect into the app, and that's it. The report is submitted. Expensify manages the remainder of the expense-filing process on the executive's behalf.

Immediately, the Expensify mobile app scans the receipt. From the image, Expensify's optical recognition lifts the name of the establishment and the amount of the transaction. Using the merchant's name and address, Expensify categorizes the expense as a restaurant. Then, the software evaluates the expense to ensure it meets the compliance requirements set by the CFO's office. Is the amount within the limits set? Is there a receipt? A few seconds later, the expense report is automatically approved, having passed the automated checks. If the credit card is the salesperson's own, Expensify schedules a bank transfer for reimbursement the next morning. Just take a photo and Expensify handles the rest.

David Barrett, Expensify's founder and product-driven CEO, maintains a singular focus to ensure Expensify's products are as simple to use as possible. This passion for simplicity extends to data analysis.

At one Expensify board meeting in 2010, I remember suggesting the company conduct a particular analysis. And David responded, quite rightly, "What decisions would that analysis inform?" In other words, the answers wouldn't have led to a change in the product roadmap or design. The metric and trends might in and of themselves be interesting, but they wouldn't have corresponded to any immediate action.

Sometimes the actionability of a metric isn't revealed until the analysis is fully completed. In his User Experience Week talk, Facebook director of product management Adam Mosseri explained how Facebook evaluates changes to its website and mobile apps, products used by more than 1 billion people each day.[8]

---

[8]Adam Mosseri, "Data Informed, Not Data Driven," *UX Week 2010*, September 28, 2010. Retrieved from https://www.youtube.com/watch?v=bKZiXAFeBeY.

Facing a competitive threat from a startup company called Quora, a question-and-answer site, and seeking to push further into search to compete with Google, Facebook launched the Questions product. Designed to enable users to ask questions on the home page, the Questions product would catalog responses from friends in poll format to provide an answer to "Which Italian restaurant in the East Village is best?" or "Who is your favorite *Glee* character?"

After launch, the Questions product wasn't generating the engagement the team had hoped for. So, the user experience (UX) team tested a variety of different versions of the Status bar, the iconic text box at the top of the Facebook news feed that prompts users with "What's on your mind?"

But the team needed to balance an increase in Questions engagement with a reduction in other interactions like uploading photos, videos, and links. After testing eight different permutations of the user interface, the UX team concluded none of the variations improved user engagement rates. So, the team decided not to change the status bar. The experiment yielded inaction because it disproved the hypothesis that a change in user interface would substantially increase Questions engagement.

The Expensify and Facebook examples differ in an important way. The UX team at Facebook tested an a priori hypothesis that updating the user interface would significantly increase user engagement. My question at the Expensify board meeting did not.

Adam Mosseri confirmed Facebook performs the two types of statistical analysis: confirmatory and exploratory data analysis. The news feed story exemplifies confirmatory data analysis. Had the team searched for a reason why users weren't engaging with Questions as much as expected, they would have been exploring data in search of hypothesis, the second type of data analysis. Often, they go hand-in-hand. Perhaps the UX team might have tested hypotheses suggested in the exploratory sessions, and A/B tested them, using the confirmatory analysis to decide which to push into the next release of the software. A/B testing, also called split testing or bucket testing, is a method of comparing two versions of a webpage or app against each other to determine which one performs better.

The importance of establishing actionability is just as important in each individual team, like the user experience team at Facebook, as it is for the executive team of a company. A relentless focus on a key metric can engender massive performance improvements to a business.

Netsuite is a $7 billion business by market capitalization with about $600 million in 2014 revenue. Larry Ellison, founder and CEO of Oracle, cofounded Netsuite in 1998 with a former Oracle employee, Evan Goldberg. The company provides enterprise resource planning (ERP) software to mid-market companies to manage procurement, revenue recognition, human capital management, and inventory management.

Netsuite's CFO Ron Gill has used the lifetime value of a customer / cost of customer acquisition (LTV/CAC) ratio to dramatically improve the business's performance. LTV/CAC is often used to justify marketing and sales investment to acquire customers. But there's much more to it.

The lifetime value of a customer (LTV) is a projection of the total future gross profit from that customer plus all the past gross profit. Gross profit is equal to revenue minus cost of goods sold. For companies who serve customers that use their product only once, the LTV is equal to the average revenue per customer. For other companies, including companies like Netsuite, who may provide software for a decade to their customers, the lifetime value of a customer can be many times their initial purchase.

The cost of customer acquisition (CAC) sums the amounts of sales and marketing investment required to acquire a single customer. It is often calculated by adding the total sales and marketing spend in the preceding period and dividing by the number of newly acquired customers in the current period. This admittedly crude measure can be improved through marketing and sales attribution, which seeks to allocate sales and marketing costs and initiatives to individual accounts on a more granular basis.

The LTV/CAC ratio marks how efficiently a company can acquire a dollar of revenue. No viable company can exist with an LTV of lower than 1. It would imply that a business uses all the future gross profit simply to acquire new customers, leaving it without the cash needed to pay rent or salaries. Businesses with very high LTV/CAC, which can range from 5 to more than 20, pay relatively little to acquire future gross profits from customers.

In the past few years, Netsuite's LTV/CAC ratio has more than doubled (an impressive feat given the stage of the business). In the

2009–2011 period, to mitigate customer churn and increase the LTV/CAC, the company invested heavily in reducing the number of customers leaving Netsuite for other products.[9]

At some point in 2011, the company couldn't squeeze any more juice from that lemon. Companies churned from Netsuite because they went out of business or were acquired, not because they selected a competitor.

So Netsuite changed tactics, and instead pursued a larger target customer to siphon business from SAP, their competitor up-market. As Netsuite has moved up-market, the larger average revenue per customer has improved the LTV/CAC because each new customer generates a much larger gross profit stream.

To identify the most important contributors impacting the LTV/CAC, Netsuite performs a regression on the underlying variables. Afterwards, the company calculates the ratio's sensitivity to each variable to understand the potential improvement attainable by focusing on reducing hosting costs, for example. These analyses lead to a set of priorities for the business that will ultimately improve LTV/CAC. This is classic confirmatory statistics.

Tracking the metric over time provides companies with an indicator for the health of the business. But because the LTV/CAC ratio is a composite number that encapsulates many other key figures, it shouldn't be used as the exclusive measure for the health of the business, but as an instrument to question the underlying dynamics, as those contributing factors can change the LTV/CAC ratio dramatically.

Understanding the major drivers of this metric, the contributions of each team, and the sensitivity to investments in particular departments is a great way to prioritize internal growth and retention efforts for marketing teams.

Regardless of the type of analysis a team performs, to be truly useful, the data must inform an action. Change the user experience. Shut down a product. Launch a new marketing campaign. Evolve the sales cycle. Actionability is a key attribute of useful data.

---

[9]S. Kupor, "Why SaaS Revenue Is Worth More Than Traditional Software Sales," A16z Podcast, March 15, 2015. Retrieved from http://a16z.com/2015/05/15/a16z-podcast-why-saas-revenue-is-worth-more-than-traditional-software-sales/.

Defining New Opportunities by Creating New Metrics That Matter

Often when determining the right metrics to measure a team's performance, the team must develop new metrics. Sometimes, new metrics must be invented because the old ones become outdated, outmoded, and inaccurate.

UPENDING THE LENDING BUSINESS

Matt Humphrey matriculated at Carnegie Mellon at age 13 to study computer science. Fifteen years later, Matt founded his seventh startup. The first three included creating interactive virtual environments to power 3-D online shopping, a peer-to-peer video delivery system delivered in a browser, and software accelerators for home routers.

Matt's first major success was a company called HomeRun, a local offers platforming content network that Rearden Commerce acquired for more than $100 million.

Meanwhile, James Herbert had graduated from Stanford with an undergraduate degree and an MBA before working for a few years at Morgan Stanley. He then decided to pursue a career in real estate. In his first year at Colony Capital, the third-largest private equity real estate fund in the world, which is reported to manage $30 billion, James acquired 5,000 homes across the United States. James bought these homes to remodel them and sell them, or as it's known in the industry, fix and flip. During this process, James struggled to find lenders who would finance these acquisitions.

At about the same time, Matt called him asking for help in evaluating an investment in a real estate fund. Over dinner, they chatted about the real estate industry. James shared his struggles. Matt was looking to start a new business, and so the two resolved to build a business together to transform lending.

In 2013, they founded LendingHome, a new financial services marketplace that provides mortgages to consumers looking to buy homes, landlords looking to buy homes and rent them, and real estate professionals fixing and flipping properties.

Two years later, LendingHome has lent more than $100 million to consumers and real estate professionals in these three categories.

In order to support that growth, the company has swelled from two people to more than 150 and raised more than $100 million in venture capital.

Unlike other lenders, which often require 30 days to fund a loan, LendingHome provides borrowers a custom quote in three minutes and wires money in less than 10 days through an entirely online process.

At the heart of LendingHome's success is a novel risk-scoring system. When lenders decide to extend a mortgage to a borrower, they must predict the risk of default, the odds that the borrower will not be able to repay the loan. Because LendingHome sells a new type of mortgage, to people who fix and flip, they couldn't copy an existing pricing model; they had to create their own.

James and Matt hired Justin Palmer, an affable native of Arkansas, as VP of data. A graduate of Brown University, Justin is a data scientist with a passion for machine learning. To inform LendingHome's model, Justin needed to create models to answer two questions. First, to which borrowers should LendingHome lend? Second, what cash flows should the lenders on LendingHome's platform expect?

So, LendingHome couldn't use the traditional FICO score, a measure of creditworthiness ranging from 300 to 850 that was introduced by the Fair Isaac Corporation in 1989. The FICO score didn't accurately measure the creditworthiness of LendingHome's borrowers. If they could create a better risk-scoring model even for traditional borrowers, they would have a long-term, sustainable competitive advantage in the mortgage business.

Unlike in the traditional mortgage market, where borrower might sign a 30-year loan and pay it off incrementally over those three decades, developers in the fix-and-flip market might repay the loan at any time. These developers use the loan to finance the remodel of the house and then sell the property when it makes sense for them.

This uncertainty presented a challenge to LendingHome. The company needed to ensure that it was meeting regulatory requirements. At the same time, it needed to lend as much money as possible in order to maximize profits.

Justin trained machine learning models across 50 million data points to predict the expected return on investment for these new types of borrowers. These new models and metrics enable the company to provide lenders an instant price for their loan and have helped the company scale loan origination rapidly.

But, LendingHome's metrics advantage doesn't stop at the online sign-up flow. Behind the scenes at every mortgage lender, mortgage officers perform more than 100 different steps in an underwriting process, from flood inspection to title search. Not content to innovate only on the quoting process, James and Matt sought to accelerate underwriting, too.

Justin built workflow tools that track the performance of the underwriting team in achieving a 10-day mortgage close target. Every morning, underwriters log into Looker, which shows them the outstanding items for upcoming mortgages, which can vary according to the regulations of each state.

LendingHome has developed new metrics to predict the creditworthiness of borrowers and accelerate the underwriting process. These models and metrics ensure that LendingHome is faster than the competition and prices risk more effectively.

The Fastest Growing Media Site of All Time

Upworthy is an online media site founded in 2012 by Eli Pariser, the former executive director of MoveOn, and Peter Koechley, the former managing editor of the satirical online publication *The Onion*. Upworthy's stated mission is to host the intersection of the "awesome," the "meaningful," and the "visual."

In 2013, Fast Company anointed Upworthy the fastest-growing media site of all time. Every day, Upworthy editors curate hundreds of stories to share with their 27 million monthly visitors.

The online publishing world measures the size and quality of its audience using page views and time on site, metrics that have been used since the very earliest days of online advertising. Unfortunately, neither one of these metrics accurately captures the true engagement of the user with content.

Imagine you're reading the *New York Times* and you receive a telephone call. While your computer might remain on that article for

25 minutes as you reminisce with an old college friend, your attention is elsewhere. Meanwhile, traditional web analytics tally those 25 minutes as engaged time. This figure is misleading for journalists who aim to measure reader satisfaction through time on site. Without an accurate metric to help them understand how different posts resonate with their audience, the Upworthy editorial team had no worthwhile compass.

So, Upworthy's data team created a new metric, attention minutes.[10] Instead of measuring the total number of people who viewed an article or the number of times readers shared the link on social media, Upworthy developed a metric to measure true user attention. Attention minutes count the amount of time users engage with the content on their pages. Instead of just looking at the basic metric of time on site, which measures the amount of time between when a user arrives on a page and when he closes the window, Upworthy's attention metric uses other signals like which browser tab is currently open, what the mouse is doing, and whether a video is playing on the page.

When the data team performed the analysis, they compared three different pieces that all had an equivalent number of pages, but discovered that the total attention minutes varied by factor of greater than three across them.

Upworthy uses attention minutes to inform both their strategy and their tactics. Total attention on site is a global metric the company uses to understand how all of their efforts are faring. Much more granular, total attention per piece helps editors and curators understand the most effective tactics for content creation and curation.

Both of these businesses have deployed innovative metrics to transform their industries. Upworthy and LendingHome have developed new metrics to provide them a sustainable competitive advantage in both of their markets.

---

[10]"What Uniques and Pageviews Leave Out (And Why ...)," *Upworthy Insider*, February 6, 2014. Retrieved from http://blog.upworthy.com/post/75795679502/what-uniques-and-pageviews-leave-out-and-why.

How to Run a Data-Backed Experiment: Step by Step

This section steps through best practices for conducting your first data-backed experiment.

STEP 1: DETERMINE ACTIONABILITY AND MERIT

Before starting an analysis and investing the time and effort required to attain the result, we should determine the actionability of the metric. What decision will the data inform? And how important is that decision relative to other decisions?

STEP 2: BOOKEND THE ANALYSIS AND TIE METRICS TO OUTCOMES

Once we agree on the merit of the analysis, before beginning to analyze the data, it's critical to bookend our expected results. As Colin Zima, the chief product officer at Looker, explains, "This is one of the keys to ensure rigor around decision-making." For example, if the Zendesk Net Promoter Score of new customers falls below 50, we should investigate our sales techniques to ensure the sales team isn't overpromising during sales pitches.

These bookended parameters should be circulated with the teams who will ultimately decide, in this case the sales and marketing teams at Zendesk. Prefacing an experiment with these experimental bounds clarifies the impact of the analysis before it's completed, helping to ensure the team uses data to decide, even if the conclusions seem counterintuitive.

STEP 3: DESIGN THE EXPERIMENT

When we create a statistical experiment, we often develop a hypothesis: If we ask for users' e-mail addresses when they sign up, we can substantially increase the number of e-mails we collect from users of our mobile application.

In statistics, like in other aspects of life, it's useful to have a devil's advocate. In this case, the devil's advocate would say that any increase in the number of collected e-mails is due to other factors. In statistics, we call the devil's advocate the null hypothesis.

The experiment should be designed to collect as much data as necessary to achieve statistical significance. Statistical significance is a concept from hypothesis testing. To ensure that the conclusion is valid, we need to gather a sufficient number of data points. Statistical significance proves the devil's advocate is wrong within a certain degree of certainty.

The most common measure of statistical significance is the p-value. The p-value is the probability that the devil's advocate is correct, assuming the data was collected well. The smaller the p-value, the greater the statistical confidence that our hypothesis is correct. Statisticians broadly have settled upon the target value of 0.05, a 5 percent chance that the devil's advocate is correct.

Sir Ronald Fisher, a British biologist who studied genetics and natural selection, developed the p-value test, and in his book *Statistical Methods for Research Workers*, published in 1925, he used a target p-value of 0.05. But, as Jason Maynard, director of data and analytics as Zendesk says, "We often have to coax our teams to accept a larger p-value, something like 0.2. Otherwise, the experiments would take too long to be useful because we would need to aggregate a much larger sample size."

Typically, the greater number of data points collected in the experiment, the smaller the potential p-value. But, each incremental data point requires time to collect, and at some point, speed is more important than marginal confidence.

To calculate the sample size for a particular experiment, use this equation:

$$Sample\ Size = \frac{1.28^2 * 0.5 * (1 - 0.5)}{0.05^2} = 163.8$$

FIGURE 8.2 Formula for Sample Size Required to Achieve Statistical Significance

Let's quickly run through the elements of the equation in Figure 8.2. Note: This equation is for an unknown or very large population size.

The Z score is determined by the desired p-value / confidence interval. Let's choose an 80 percent confidence interval. The Z score is 1.28.

The standard of deviation is measured on a scale from 0 to 1. Most people use 0.5 since it is the most forgiving value and will generate the largest sample size. See Figure 8.3.

P-Value	Confidence Level	Z-Score
0.01	99%	2.58
0.05	95%	1.96
0.10	90%	1.65
0.20	80%	1.28
0.30	70%	1.04

FIGURE 8.3 Z-Score Table

The margin of error is also called the confidence interval. See Figure 8.4. When a political poll says a candidate commands 19 percent of the vote +/– 5 percent, the 5 percent is the margin of error. Let's use 5 percent.

Sample Size

$$= \frac{Z\ Score^2 * Standard\ of\ Deviation * (1 - Standard\ of\ Deviation)}{Margin\ of\ Error^2}$$

FIGURE 8.4 Sample Size Calculation for 80% Confidence

So, to have 80 percent confidence with a 5 percent margin of error, we need 164 samples. A 99 percent confidence with a 5 percent margin of error requires 666 samples, more than three times the number of data points.

STEP 4: CALCULATE THE TIME REQUIRED TO RUN THE EXPERIMENT

At this point, we know precisely the number of samples we need in order to attain a satisfactory result for the experiment. Now, we can calculate the amount of time required to run the experiment. Typically experiments on websites and mobile applications are run using A/B tests, where a fraction of the total traffic and users are diverted to a particular experiment. Let's suppose in this case, we have 10,000 active users per day and the product team allows us to divert 2 percent of traffic to this experiment. Two percent of 10,000 active users is 200 users. Running an experiment with 164 samples requires only one day.

Time to speak with the engineers about instrumenting the experiment and pushing it into production.

Step 5: Run the Experiment and Analyze the Results

After the experiment has been run, aggregate the results and analyze the results, using a t-test or similar to determine if there's a substantial difference in the value between the experimental and control groups.

This five-step process, though simple, when consistently executed will ensure a team is asking the right questions; investing time identifying meaningful, important, and actionable decisions; and engendering support for the right decision, even if the data contradicts the expectations of the teams involved.

Chapter 9

Changing the Way We Operate

Change Begins with a Story

To hell with facts! We need stories!

—Ken Kesey

In its simplest form, a story is a connection between cause and effect. Peter tricks the villagers too many times with a false "Wolf" cry. For his transgression, he suffers the loss of his flock. When Aesop wrote his fables, he inculcated in Greek children a sense of cause-and-effect relationships that would serve them all their lives.

Like those morals, the implications of data are best conveyed through stories. At a TedX talk in New York, Ben Wellington explained how he came to call himself a data storyteller. Ben is trained in data science and his wife works as an urban planner. In 2012, New York City mayor Michael Bloomberg signed a law granting public access to all urban planning data to citizens through a website. Ben applied his skills to reveal the trends in urban planning. And, with an expert at home, he produced insightful analysis quickly.[1]

The New York City government data set contains parking ticket history, bicycle accidents, and taxi pickup and drop-off times and places, among other things. Ben pulled the data and began to pick it apart. In 2013, he published his first analysis: a map of cycling injuries across the five boroughs. Ben published it on his blog, I Quant NY. Many other news outlets syndicated his analysis and traffic ballooned.

---

[1]B. Wellington, "Making Data Mean More through Storytelling," *TEDxBroadway*, April 20, 2015. Retrieved from https://www.youtube.com/watch?v=6xsvGYIxJok.

Reflecting on his success, Ben realized that his lifelong passion for improvisational comedy, a hobby from age 13, influenced his storytelling style. First, Ben emphasizes the importance of connecting people's existing experiences with data. By enabling an audience to relate to the data, the speaker can maximize its impact. Ben frames his pharmacy analysis of Manhattan as a giant game of Risk. Duane Reade, a well-known Manhattan pharmacy chain, dominates the center of the island, while the competition threatens the castle. CVS attacks from New Jersey and Rite Aid descends from the Bronx.

Second, visualizations must focuses on one idea that highlights an interesting pattern. In one of his analyses, Ben charts the gender distribution of people riding Citi Bikes. Citi Bikes is a bike-sharing program in New York City sponsored by the international bank Citi. It has been a huge success. Riders booked more than 1 million rides in August 2014 on a fleet of 5,000 bicycles.[2]

But, there are regional differences in ridership. The further north a city bike station is placed, the greater the likelihood the rider is male. And as Ben quips in his talk, "If you're looking to meet a girl on a Citi Bike, go to Brooklyn."

Last, Ben emphasizes the important of making an impact. He analyzed the parking ticket revenue created by each fire hydrant in Manhattan and discovered that two fire hydrants in the Lower East Side generated more than $55,000 annually in parking tickets.

Using Google Maps, Ben uncovered the reason traffic officers were ticketing so many cars in that area. It was an unusual parking spot. Instead of abutting the curb, a bike lane separated the parking space from the sidewalk pierced by a black NYC fire hydrant.

The New York City Department of Transportation had painted lines for a parking spot, ostensibly blessing it. But, the local police department, which enforces the parking code and writes the tickets, had deemed the spot to be illegal because of the hydrant. All the conflicting signals confused drivers who parked there. But the local precinct ticketed. Ben wrote the Department of Transportation, and within a few days, the parking spot was repainted as a no-parking zone.

---

[2]"NYCBS August 2014 Monthly Report," Citi Bike NYC, August 2014. Retrieved from https://www.citibikenyc.com/assets/pdf/august_2014_citi_bike_monthly_report.pdf

This combination of reporting and data has a name: computational journalism. Journalists are powerful, convincing storytellers who can harness the power of data to convey their story with new meaning.

Benjamin Morris, a writer for arguably the best computational journalism publication, *fivethirtyeight*, published "Lionel Messi Is Impossible,"[3] which describes in words, statistics, and charts why Lionel Messi is one of the greatest players in the world (see Figure 9.1).

In their Group F World Cup match late last month, Argentina and Iran were still deadlocked after 90 minutes. With the game in stoppage time and the score tied at 0–0, Lionel Messi took the ball near the right corner of the penalty area, held it for a moment, then broke left, found his seam, took his strike, and curled it in from 29 yards. What was going to be a draw was now a win, and Messi had put Argentina into the Round of 16.

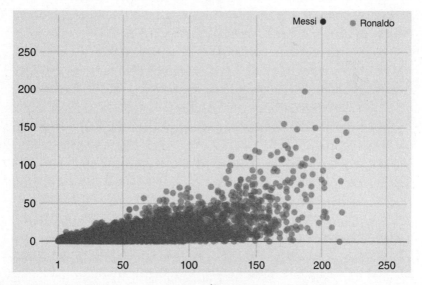

FIGURE 9.1 Overall Scoring Production (Total goals and assists versus games played since 2010 World Cup)

---

[3]B. Morris, "Lionel Messi Is Impossible," FiveThirtyEight, July 1, 2014. Retrieved http://fivethirtyeight.com/features/lionel-messi-is-impossible/.

I think it's fair to say that goals mean more in soccer than points do in most sports. And Messi scores a lot of them. Since the end of the 2010 World Cup, Messi has been responsible for 291 goals and assists in 201 of his games in club and national team play, tracked by the sports analytics company Opta. How does that compare with other soccer stars across top leagues around the world?

Morris's article is superb for three reasons. First, each chart succinctly conveys a single point. The charts are simple, but the analysis underpinning them is not. Achieving that simplicity from complexity isn't easy.

Second, the data presents a clear and consistent story. Each plot depicts Messi's exceptional performance as a striker compared to his peers. Without such an exceptional career and statistics, this story would have been far less compelling. In other words, the data clearly supports the narrative.

Third, Morris openly discusses the blind spots of each analysis and has anticipated the readers' questions himself, which is a terrific way of managing doubt. Two-thirds of the way through the article, for example, Morris changes the analysis from Messi the individual to Messi the team player: "By this point, it should be evident that Messi has at least a little bit of skill. But there's still heavy lifting to do: We have to show that he actually makes his team better."

In both of these examples, the analysts and authors create a connection with the audience by using data to illustrate a point.

One of the leading experts in the world on delivering presentations, Nancy Duarte, is the CEO of Duarte Design, the largest design firm in Silicon Valley. She has worked with many prominent speakers, including Al Gore on his expository presentation on global warming, *An Inconvenient Truth*.

Duarte has written three books on presentations, including one called *Resonate*, which is available free online at www.duarte.com/book/resonate/. *Resonate* dissects iconic speeches and presentations including Steve Jobs's announcement of the iPhone, Richard Feynman's lecture on gravity, and Martin Luther King's "I Have a Dream" speech.

In each of these case studies, Duarte enumerates the components of the speech that make it so memorable, from the emotional tension to the diction, from the data to the delivery: "Even with mountains of facts, you can still fail to resonate. That is because resonance doesn't come from the information itself, but rather from the emotional impact of that information. This doesn't mean that you should abandon facts entirely. Use plenty of facts, but accompany them with emotional appeal. There's a difference between being convinced with logic and believing with personal conviction."[4]

Data alone is not powerful enough to inspire people to act or change. It must be interwoven with passion and emotion and conviction. By becoming great storytellers with data, we can change the way our businesses operate.

Deliver Data with Panache: Structuring Presentations to Inspire

For most people, presentations will be the predominant medium they use to communicate points with data. Prevalent in meetings across the world, presentations certainly have their drawbacks, but when used properly, they can be incredibly effective storytelling mechanisms, especially when the story is supported by data.

When startup companies seek to raise venture capital, the predominant pitch medium is the presentation. Historically, founders have presented their pitch decks in 60-minute meetings with venture capital partners. Today, those meetings still form the basis of most fund-raising processes, but they are complemented by shorter presentations.

YCombinator, the preeminent incubator and institutional seed investment firm based in Mountain View, CA, popularized the idea of Demo Days. On Demo Day, more than fifty startup founders will present their business to a horde of venture capitalists and angel investors in about 2 minutes. It's the clichéd elevator pitch.

In both Demo Day and classical pitches, the entrepreneur's goal is to engender a sense of urgency to invest in the business: that the team has identified a new opportunity that will address a multibillion-dollar market and create an enduring and category-defining business.

---

[4]N. Duarte, *Resonate: Present Visual Stories That Transform Audiences* (Hoboken, NJ: John Wiley & Sons, 2010), 19.

Step 1: Define the Objective

First, it's essential to define the goal of the presentation. Are you looking to inform someone and solicit feedback on a particular topic? Or is the point of the presentation to convince someone to act in a particular way? The presentation may be an opportunity to argue for an investment in a new product, the cessation of a particular marketing campaign, or a novel experiment in sales compensation. Whatever it is, understanding exactly where you want to leave the audience is the first ingredient for success. For startups raising capital, the presentation aims to convince investors that the rewards of investing in this business far outweigh the risks.

Step 2: Understand the Audience

Next, it's essential to understand the audience. Investors will want to know many things about a business before writing a check. Venture capitalists seek to understand the risks facing a startup. There are 11 different risk types investors often diligence before investing.

1. **Market timing risk**—Is now the right time for the business? What technologies or market discontinuities suddenly create the opportunity for this startup to succeed?
2. **Business model risk**—Is there a clear business model that will sustain an enduring business? Do the unit economics work? What must be assumed for the company to attain profitability?
3. **Market adoption risk**—Have consumers/customers expressed a strong interest in using/buying the startup's product? Are there fearsome incumbents in the market? If so, what is the likely competitive response? What are the major barriers to entry in this sector?
4. **Market size risk**—If the company is successful, is the exit scenario large enough to provide the types of returns a venture capitalist seeks?
5. **Execution risk**—Does the team have the right skills and passion to reach their goals? If not, are they amenable to finding others to complement their skills?

6. Technology risk—Will the company attempt to develop a new, experimental technology? How likely will the development effort for or require substantially more time than projected?

7. Capitalization structure risk—Does the company have the ability to raise sufficient capital to achieve its vision?

8. Platform risk—Does the business depend on a key partner to grow? Is the startup building atop YouTube, Twitter, Facebook, Salesforce, Slack, or another distribution platform? How strong is the relationship between the platform and the startup? Are their product plans competitive or complementary?

9. Venture management risk—Is the company receptive to feedback? Is the team candid about the state of the business and their own strengths and weaknesses?

10. Financial risk—How much money does the company require to achieve its goals? Will the company be able to attain meaningful milestones on the current amount invested to raise the next tranche of capital? Is the financing risk manageable given the current environment and company trajectory?

11. Legal risk—Does the company have a high likelihood of lawsuit for patent or copyright infringement? Does the company have any outstanding complaints with early employees or founders? Are there regulatory challenges involved in this sector?

STEP 3: CREATE THE ARC OF THE STORY

Having understood the risks venture investors seek to address in pitch meetings, it's time to craft the storyline. While there are many different techniques to tell stories, there does seem to be a consistent pattern in the structure of successful pitch decks.

DocSend, a San Francisco based startup, partnered with Harvard Business School professor Tom Eisenmann to analyze the pitch decks of 200 companies that collectively raised more than $360M.[5] Their

---

[5]"What We Learned From 200 Startups Who Raised $360M," DocSend, June 18, 2015. Retrieved from https://docsend.com/view/p8jxsqr.

analysis showed 10 slides is the optimal length for fundraising pitches. Based upon their data, they recommend the pitch articulate the story in the following order:

Company Purpose: the mission or goal of the business

1. Problem: the complication with the status quo that creates the opportunity for the business to pursue
2. Solution: the company's proposed idea to resolve the problem
3. Why Now: why should this idea succeed now, when no one has succeeded with it before?
4. Market Size: if the business were to succeed, how valuable could it be?
5. Product: typically, a demonstration of the product or images of the technology
6. Team: the members of the founding and executive team, often including key advisors and investors
7. Business Model: an overview of the business' pricing strategy and unit economics.
8. Competition: a description of the alternatives and substitutes and how the startup intends to differentiate itself
9. Financials: a pro-forma profit and loss projection of the business. In Docsend's analysis, investors spend the most time on this slide to understand the long-term profitability of the business and the amount of capital required to sustain the company.

STEP 4: AMASS THE DATA

In these ten slides, founders communicate a compelling vision of the opportunity before the business. Data often reinforces three of these slides: Solution, Market Size, and Financials

Solution The Solution slide often explains the company's approach and the market's reception to the product. Founders often present two different types of metrics to assert their solution is the best: engagement metrics and acquisition metrics.

Engagement metrics including daily active users and monthly active users articulate the value users place on the service. If 75% of the users of a product log in every day and use it for several hours, clearly the team has developed a product that rivals the most successful social networks of the day. In addition, engagement metrics also illustrate the longevity of the user. Do users play with a product for a few weeks and then skip to the next thing, or do they persist their activity for months?

Engagement metrics prelude revenue metrics. For example, in 2004, Facebook counted 1 million users and generated $400,000 in revenue. Eleven years later, the company counted 1.4 billion users and generated $17.9 billion in revenue. The average revenue generated per user in that time period grew by 32x.

Acquisition metrics reveal the costs to acquire customer and the revenue generated per customer in a given time frame. Software companies often report several metrics. The sales cycle measured in days indicates how quickly the company can convince a prospect to sign a contract to use the software. The most compelling software often record sales cycles of less than 30 days.

Sales efficiency measures the amount of sales and marketing dollars the company needs to invest in one quarter to generate one dollar of gross margin in the subsequent quarter. Also called the magic number, sales efficiency typically hovers around one, but the most efficient companies can sustain ratios of 1.1–1.3 for extended periods of time.

Cost of customer acquisition payback: when selling software, a company must invest ahead of the sale by marketing their solution and also hiring account executives to sell it. As the customer pays for the software, the company recoups this investment over time. The average software company requires 11 months to recoup their investment.

There are other metrics to convey the inevitable success of the start up, But these are the most common.

Market Size Market size ranks among venture capitalists' first questions about a startup investment opportunity because the successful startups in the investor's portfolio must be large enough to pay for all the money lost in failed startups, and generate attractive returns.

There are many different investment strategies venture investors can pursue. Figure 9.2 contrasts two funds, one $50M and one $500M fund. Both target a return of 3x over 10 years for their

	$50M fund	$500M fund
Target Return Multiple	3	3
Implied Portfolio Holding Value	$150M	$1,500M
Average Ownership	10%	25%
Total Market Cap of Portfolio	$1,500M	$6,000M
Avg Investment Size Including Reserves	2.5M	$10M
Number of Investments per Fund	20	50
Company Failure Rate	50%	70%
Successful Investments	10	15
Avg Market Cap of Exit	$150M	$400M

FIGURE 9.2   Sample Fund Return Strategies for a $50M and $500M Venture Fund

investors. The $50M fund typically owns 10 percent of the startup when at acquisition or IPO, while the bigger fund owns 25 percent. To attain the target return, the total market capitalization of each fund must be 4x its size (1x to payback the dollars raised and 3x to attain the target). If 50–70 percent of startups fail and the average investment sizes are the ones indicated above, then the first fund must average $150M price on the sale or IPO of its 10 successful companies. The larger fund must exit its positions at $400M on average. Most of the time, three to four companies in each fund generate the vast majority of the returns.

This power law dynamic in venture capital returns, where a handful of companies return enough money to offset an investor's losses, pushes venture capitalists to chase very large opportunities, which by their nature create or win share in massive markets.

To be worth $1B, a software company might need to generate $100M in annual revenue and be growing by 50%+ annually. At this point, the company represents 5-10% of the total market implying $1–2 billion in observed revenues. And that's roughly the market size target of most venture capitalists with multi-hundred million dollar funds.

The market size segment of a startup's presentation argues the opportunity before the business could be worth many billions of dollars in revenue. Founders often communicate this in two ways: top-down and bottom-up.

A top-down TAM (Total Addressable Market) analysis for a hypo-thetical sales software company would estimate a 0.25% addressable market from a total enterprise software spend of $620B annually to reach $2.4B. The 0.25% is estimated by the company.

A bottom-up TAM calculation multiplies the roughly 4M sales-people in the US from the US Business Census, and an average price point of $50 per person per month for the startup's software. The TAM: $2.4 Billion.

Financials   The financial slide is a critical component of the pitch deck. Most founders present a combination of the Net Income Statement and a Cashflow statement. The most important figures for venture investor are:

- ◆ Revenue: how quickly can accompany scale its revenues?
- ◆ Gross margin: how much margin can the company generate and its business? More margin implies the company can invest substantially more in sales and marketing and research and development, to grow the business faster and also develop new products.
- ◆ Burn: how much cash does the company need to breach cash flow breakeven and net income profitability?

STEP 5: DELIVER THE PRESENTATION

Whether delivering the pitch at a Demo Day or at the offices of a venture capitalist, start of founders will be peppered with questions. What fraction of your users originates from search engine optimiza-tion? How has the average revenue per user increased over time? How many customers must close next month in order to achieve the company's bookings goals?

The most impressive founders are able to respond to those queries with data. In addition to answering the questions effectively, these data-driven founders demonstrate supreme command of their businesses and will continue to lead, guide, and decide effectively.

Chapter 10

Putting It All Together

C hange today is more complex, faster, and harder to predict than ever before. Consequently, competition in business has never been more demanding. The only antidote to this increasing volatility is data.

Every industry will be transformed by data. Perhaps the Madison Avenue Mad Men were the first to suffer the disruption introduced by the analysis of ones and zeros, but they certainly won't be the last. Uber assailed the taxicab industry and felled a decades-old, iconic yellow-taxi business in San Francisco in just a few years, without owning a single taxicab.

Disruptors, like Uber, deploy data supply chains that nourish data cultures. Within these crucibles, data democracy thrives. Managers of retail stores use data to maximize customer satisfaction, introducing hand sanitizer in the winter at Warby Parker. Merchandisers at The RealReal change their inventory and optimize their marketing techniques at 4 p.m. to ensure that every day the business achieves its revenue target.

Operationalizing data, using data to improve the business's performance, will be the defining competitive advantage of the future. No longer are we using data to evaluate our trajectory in the rearview mirror. Instead, new data infrastructures powered by next-generation databases and data-exploration tools expose information to the people on the front lines, how and when they need it to decide—in minutes, not weeks.

This unquenchable thirst for data is a cultural change at a global level, caused by the ubiquity of the cell phone. We can ask and answer questions in seconds by querying a search engine or sending a text message in our personal lives. But at work, we are challenged by the invisible data breadlines, the data brawls within our meetings, the fragmentation of our data across a company, and the lack of consistency across metrics and data points.

Friction. Friction everywhere. Without an ability to analyze dispassionately, argue over facts, or run quick and incisive experiments, friction permeates our meetings. Today, we grease these conversations using opinion, gut, instinct, intuition, or apathy. Without data, seniority wins. Without an ability to suggest an idea, influence the team's course of action, or design an experiment to test the hypothesis, most people in a meeting room don't contribute. Data provides us the perspective we need to curtail conversations about bike racks and other trivialities.

With modern data infrastructure, we can shed the rust, liberate the collective curiosity of our teams, and change the way our companies innovate in industry.

Of course, the technology itself is necessary but insufficient. Modern data supply chains must be married to a group of people who seek data, who speak data, and who demand data when making decisions.

Brutal intellectual honesty underpins all data-centric cultures. Dominic Orr, former CEO of Aruba, articulated the strength necessary to demand total honesty. Team members have to be able to separate their ego from the decision-making process. When a company or team decides to pursue only the best ideas regardless of who proposed them or who has championed them in the past, then they achieve brutal intellectual honesty.

Honesty requires the right people in the company. That process begins with defining the key values of a business. Google is perhaps most famous for its difficult-to-describe quality of Googliness, which encapsulates many different attributes—perhaps most salient, intellectual curiosity. Once defined, these values form key evaluation criteria in interviewing processes. Consequently, the recruiting team must find and hire intellectually curious employees, the ones whose insatiable appetite for understanding why and what could be can be quenched by data.

The data team, the increasingly important data team, who has been overwhelmed by the demand for data, must rise to meet a new challenge as the culture evolves and new employees push the organization forward: They must shepherd their organization.

At Facebook and Zendesk, data teams' responsibilities start with deploying modern data infrastructure. Modern data infrastructure is powered by advances in database technology that started with Google in the early 2000s. Today, that technology is available to everybody. But to access ever-increasing volumes of data, data teams and data-driven businesses need a single, unified, consistent data fabric that allows the entire company to interrogate, query, and parse data as easily as a data engineer.

More than that, data teams must be mission-driven organizations that educate their peers to use data effectively—both the tools and the analytical techniques. Data teams arbitrate the handoffs of metrics between teams, safeguarding the unified lexicon across the company.

In addition, the data team is positioned to educate people across the company on how to articulate the importance of their points and their ideas using data buttressed with stories. While data can be a powerful asset, the conviction of the speaker and the impact of the decision are powerful calls to action. As Nancy Duarte says, "Even with mountains of facts, you can still fail to resonate."

An important and nuanced part of the literacy is understanding and avoiding biases like those that plagued the U.S. Air Force. In the midst of World War II, losing more than 30 planes a day to enemy gunfire, the U.S. Air Force sought to reinforce their planes by placing additional armor over the gouges left by flak cannons in the wings and fuselages of the surviving planes. Fortunately, they were saved from their folly by a naturalized Rumanian statistician, Abraham Wald, who correctly identified the survivorship bias in their analysis and recommended instead they armor planes in the areas where surviving bombers showed no damage. For, after all, the planes that hadn't returned must have been shot there.

With this kind of support, ranging from education on tools to storytelling from the data team, teams across the company can create new metrics the way Upworthy and LendingHome have. These new metrics improve the way these business operate, providing a long-term competitive advantage.

Upworthy's use of attention minutes, rather than the traditional cost per thousand impressions, as a metric for charging advertisers aligns the incentives of readers, journalists, and advertisers. LendingHome has crafted proprietary algorithms to price risk for new mortgage product and developed workflow tools to deliver customer experience 66 percent faster than its competition.

New metrics ultimately transform internal processes. At Redpoint, we have built data systems to generate meaningful information asymmetries, which are a key competitive advantage in an industry as fierce as venture capital. In addition, we've been able to evolve the way we write content in order to develop our brand awareness and improve our business development efforts.

With a unified data fabric and a deliberate team, companies can transform themselves and their industries. We can eliminate the notion of a single librarian inundated by the monotonically increasing volume of data requests. In fact, the library industry is also being transformed by data.

In 2012, the Harvard Smithsonian Center for Astrophysics Library developed an experimental course: Data Scientist Training for Librarians.[1] The class has inspired a global community of librarians to familiarize themselves with the world of data. Long live the card catalog!

---

[1]"Registration Open for Data Scientist Training for Librarians," Harvard Library Portal, n.d. Retrieved March 15, 2016, from http://library.harvard.edu/06112015-1629/registration-open-data-scientist-training-librarians.

Acknowledgments

Thank you to my darling wife, Casey, who inspired this adventure and who sacrificed holidays, evenings, and weekends to make this book, and most everything else in our wonderful adventure together possible. Thank you also to my two boys, Henry and Thibaut, who came into my office to ask why I was working and invited me to play with their wooden train set instead. Dr. Richard McDonald and Corinne McDonald inspired new chapters and new subjects whenever the inevitable writer's block set in. My parents, my sisters and brother, for their tireless support.

At Looker: Lloyd Tabb, founder of Looker, and mentor to many, who chose Redpoint as his Series A investor. Thank you for taking a risk on me. Jen Grant took copious, helpful notes, suggested brilliant titles, and always supplied much-needed enthusiasm. Kelly Payne's encyclopedic knowledge of Looker's customers and case studies will never be replicated. Frank Bien, my co-author and literary partner.

The Redpoint team supported this effort enormously. First, Geoff Yang, who hired and trained me, the greenest person ever to join a venture capital firm. Second, Tim Haley and Jeff Brody, who championed our initial coinvestments. John Walecka, Satish Dharamarj, Scott Raney, Chris Moore, Ryan Sarver, and Jamie Davidson have provided friendship, guidance, and advice along the way. Hadley Wilkins tirelessly tuned the marketing and positioning. Natalie Bartlett selflessly volunteered to document the citations and read the first drafts. Jen Bulawsky defended the schedule so I could write.

At Wiley, Richard Narramore invited us on this journey and always challenged us to think a bit bigger.

At Google, Marissa Mayer, Susan Wojcicki, Scott Sheffer, Brian Axe, and Kim Malone showed me how great leaders lead and taught me the value of data.

Justin Palmer shared his wonderful history at LendingHome, and his love of Southern barbecue. Jason Maynard squeezed me in a few days before he set off on a grand adventure to the South of France. Jane McLaughlin contributed, edited, and organized the table of contents.

Appendix: Revenue Metrics

Business Revenue Metrics

Let's consider a hypothetical SaaS startup called RedRocket, which sells software for $12,000 per year and asks its customers to pay each quarter. On the 15th day of January, one customer agrees to pay RedRocket $12,000 for a one-year contract. The startup doesn't sell any more software for the next 12 months. The table below demonstrates the differences in bookings, monthly recurring revenue (MRR), revenue, and billings.

Month	Jan	Feb	Mar	Apr	May	Jan
ACV bookings	12,000					
MRR	1,000	1,000	1,000	1,000	1,000	0
Recognized revenue	516	1,000	1,000	1,000	1,000	484
Billings/cash collections	3000			3000		

Annual contract value bookings (ACV bookings): Bookings are the amount of money customers have committed to spend with the business. The sum total of future spend is booked in the month a customer signs a contract. Companies with only 12-month contracts can report ACV bookings; companies with other length contracts, both shorter and longer, report total contract value (TCV) bookings. Sometimes companies normalize TCV into an annual number to report ACV.

Monthly recurring revenue (MRR): The company records $1,000 in MRR in January. Recurring revenue is a metric used by subscription businesses, those companies that contract their customers over some period of time. The MRR is the annualized spend of all customers divided by 12. RedRocket reports MRR at the end of each month. So in a year, assuming the customer doesn't renew, MRR drops to zero.

Recognized revenue: The company recognizes $516 in revenue in January, which is the amortized amount for the last 16 days in January, and $1,000 in revenue each subsequent month, through the first 15 days of next January. In January next year, the company recognizes $484 in revenue. Again, this is the amortized amount for the first 15 days of January. Revenue can be recognized only for the days that RedRocket's software is provided to the customer, in this January's case, the last 16 days of the month ($16 \div 31 \times 1,000 = \$516$). This amortization of revenue and expenses across time periods is called accrual accounting.

Revenue growth is an important primary measure of the health of the business. Revenue growth is often calculated on a monthly, quarterly, and annual basis.

Billings: Billings are the amount of cash collected from customers in a given period. The company collects $3,000 of cash up front from the customer, and then again three more times during the year each quarter. RedRocket's cash collections should equal the incoming cash from customers into the company's bank accounts. Cash collections exclude financings.

Gross margin: Gross margin is equal to the revenue of the company minus its cost of goods sold (COGS). COGS include everything needed to provide a product or service to a customer, including the hosting infrastructure to deliver a website, customer support to onboard new users, raw materials in the case of manufacturing, and so on. The higher the percentage, the more money the business has to spend in other areas like sales and marketing. Gross margins vary dramatically by industry, from about 25 percent for Walmart to 85 percent for Facebook.

Net income: Also colloquially called profitability, a business's net income is the revenue minus the cost of goods sold, expenses, and taxes.

Cash burn: A company's burn is the difference in its bank accounts from one period to the next. That's the simplest way to calculate it. Because of the differences between revenue and billings, the net income and cash burn can differ wildly. A company can be cash-flow positive, meaning the business has a larger bank account this month than last month, but still be unprofitable, because the business must recognize the revenue over a year.

Unit economics: In contrast to general business metrics, which evaluate a business at the highest levels, unit economics measure a business looking at the profitability to serve just one customer. Unit economic analysis is useful to understand the trends in a particular product over time. It is especially helpful to companies projecting when they will become profitable. For example, is the business becoming better and better at acquiring customers inexpensively?

Average revenue per customer (ARPC): The ARPC is the average of the recognized revenue across all customers in a period. ARPC can vary because of many different factors, including customer geography, customer acquisition source (direct sales, online acquisition, word of mouth, referral), customer size, and customer longevity. It's a useful diagnostic metric to understand where the company is succeeding and where there might be some opportunities to grow accounts.

Contribution margin: Also called dollar contribution per unit, the contribution margin is the revenue generated for one unit of a product minus its variable costs. Variable costs are the costs incurred by a business that increase as the business makes more of its products. They include website hosting, raw materials, hourly manufacturing, and labor. On the other hand, fixed costs, like rent for an office or salaries of the executives of a company, don't fluctuate with changes in production.

Contribution margin provides an incisive understanding into how profitable a company is. A business with a 50 percent contribution margin will have 50 cents per dollar of revenue to spend on its fixed costs. The surplus is profit. A business with a negative contribution margin or a contribution margin that is lower than the fixed costs is in trouble!

Churn rate: Churn rate is the measure of the number of previous customers who have stopped paying for a product in the given period. It is typically measured in two ways, on a unit basis (the total count of customers who have churned) and a dollar basis (the percentage of revenue dollars churned).

As Figure A.1 shows, revenue churn slows the growth rate of a business. At a constant churn rate over months or years, it becomes increasingly expensive for a business to replace lost revenue from churned customers. Suppose a business records a 25 percent annual

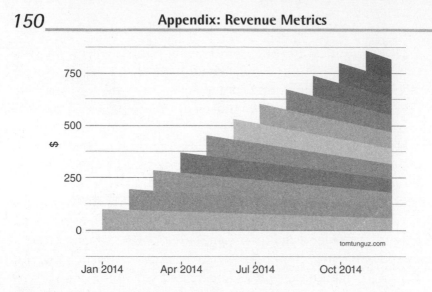

tomtunguz.com

Jan 2014   Apr 2014   Jul 2014   Oct 2014

FIGURE A.1   Account Value by Cohort at 5 Percent Churn

customer churn rate and it costs the business $2 of sales and marketing costs to acquire $1 of revenue. At $10 million in annual revenue, the business loses $2.5 million in revenue per year and must spend $5 million to replace it. At $250 million in revenue, the business loses $63 million in revenue per year and must reinvest more than $125 million.

Account expansion: Many businesses have a wide dispersion in the value of their customers. For example, the online collaboration vendor Box has acquired customers worth $120 per year and others worth more than $1.2 million per year. If Box lost 5 percent of its customers (unit churn), but they were all small customers, the trend would be worth investigating but not worrisome. However, if Box was to lose its biggest client, worth more than $10 million, then the unit churn would be low, but the dollar churn would be quite high, and the company should be concerned.

Many software companies also measure their account expansion rate. In these software companies, the revenue a customer generates changes with time. In addition to churning, these customers can pay a business more. In the case of Box, a growing business might buy more seats of Box for new employees. Growing customer accounts consistently is a very efficient way to grow.

Box generates 30 percent year over year account growth, meaning an account worth $1,000 last year on average will be worth

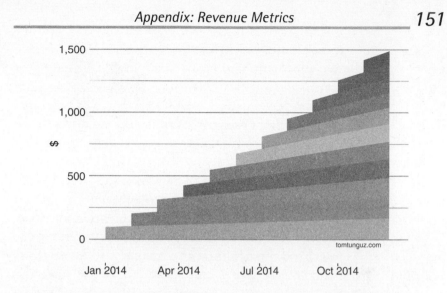

FIGURE A.2 Account Value by Cohort at 5 Percent Negative Churn

$1,300 this year. Thirty percent average account expansion is exceptional. As shown in Figure A.2, describing a hypothetical company, this account expansions effect is like a bank account, and the value of a company's revenue compounds over time.

Engagement Metrics

Qualified candidates (QCs): The equivalent of a sales qualified lead, the QC is a leading indicator of whether the team will attain its hiring goals for the quarter. A QC is defined as a phone interview that qualifies a candidate as a good fit for a requisition. By understanding the QC to accepted offer rate over time, a company can forecast the odds of attaining the hiring goal that quarter, just as sales teams estimate bookings.

Days to close: Speed is a competitive advantage in recruiting because the most sought-after candidates will have many options. Greenhouse and many other top recruiting companies maintain less than 30-day latency between first contact and signed offer.

Candidate satisfaction: After every interview, Greenhouse sends a survey to interviewees to gauge their satisfaction with the process, including how well the position was explained, how well prepared the interviewers were, and whether they felt respected and treated courteously. Startups should aim for 70 percent or better.

Offer acceptance rate: What fraction of people who receive offers accept them? This figure should be quite high, 75 percent or greater in some cases. If the offer acceptance rate is low, the recruiting team should investigate. Some causes include lower candidate satisfaction, an unduly long hiring cycle, unclear hiring parameters in the job requisition, and miscommunication between recruiting and hiring managers.

Hires to goal: The total number of new hires divided by the goal. A company that isn't achieving its hires-to-goal number should understand the bottleneck, whether in sourcing, evaluation, or close.

Regretted and not-regretted employee retention: One of the key metrics to understand the health of the human resources efforts and initiatives at a company is the rate at which people leave the business. Regretted churn is losses of employees the business would rather have retained. Nonregretted churn is terminations of existing employees who didn't work out for one reason or another.

Obviously, regretted churn should be kept to an absolute minimum. If a company observes high regretted churn, it's time to evaluate employee retention packages, delve deeper into manager/report relationships, and potentially perform an employee satisfaction survey.

Distribution Metrics
BRAND HEALTH METRICS

Aided and unaided recall: These two metrics go hand-in-hand. They measure the health of a company's brand awareness. They are usually calculated by sending out a brand awareness survey.

The survey includes questions like "What venture capital firms are you familiar with? (Please write your answers in the box below.)" Unaided recall measures the fraction of people surveyed who without prompting can name a company's brand. Unaided recall is a good proxy for the effectiveness of brand marketing campaigns. If 75 percent of respondents to the survey can name your company's brand, this indicates very strong brand health.

Aided recall asks questions like "Are you familiar with Redpoint?" These questions lower the bar for recall and indicate a good brand health, but not as strong as unaided recall.

Net Promoter Score (NPS): Bain & Co. developed the NPS in the early 2000s to measure customer loyalty. It is measured on a scale from +100 to −100 and is gathered by sending out a survey to customers asking each one, "How likely are you to recommend this product to a friend or colleague?" The recipient answers on a scale from 1 to 10. Respondents who mark 9 or 10 on the survey are Promoters. Those who mark 0 to 6 are Detractors. The remainder are dubbed Passives. The NPS is calculated by subtracting the number of Promoters from Detractors. At the bottom of the heap, companies like Time Warner Cable register −20 NPS.[1] In 2015, Costco recorded the highest NPS of all Fortune 500 companies, at 79.[2] Net Promoter Score is a good proxy for the likelihood of customers to refer other customers, indicating strong brand health.

Virality: Virality measures the number of new customers referred by existing customers over a given time period. Also called k-factor, the virality coefficient is calculated by multiplying the number of referral invitations to a product sent by each existing customer, by the percent conversion of each invite. This metric is borrowed from medicine, in particular epidemiology, which uses the same figure to measure the growth rate of a virus. A virality coefficient greater than one indicates exponential growth because one new customer refers more than one new customer.

PAID ACQUISITION METRICS

Lifetime value (LTV): The lifetime value of a customer is a projection of the total future gross profit from that customer plus all the past gross profit. Gross profit is equal to revenue minus cost of goods sold. For companies that serve customers who use their product only once, the LTV is equal to the average revenue per customer. For other companies, including companies like Netsuite, who may provide software for a decade to their customers, the lifetime value of a customer can be many times their initial purchase.

Cost of customer acquisition (CAC): The CAC sums the amounts of sales and marketing investment required to acquire a

---

[1]http://blog.satmetrix.com/2015-consumer-nps-benchmarks-study-part-iii-entertainment-telecom.
[2]www.satmetrix.com/in-the-news/costco-usaa-amazon-and-apple-rank-among-highest-in-customer-loyalty-in-latest-satmetrix-net-promoter-benchmarks/.

single customer. It is often calculated by summing the total sales and marketing spend in the preceding period and dividing by the number of newly acquired customers in the current period. This admittedly crude measure can be improved through marketing and sales attribution, which seeks to allocate sales and marketing costs and initiatives to individual accounts on a more granular basis.

LTV/CAC ratio: The LTV/CAC ratio marks how efficiently a company can acquire a dollar of revenue. No viable company can exist with an LTV of lower than 1. It would imply that a business uses all the future gross profit simply to acquire new customers, leaving it without the cash needed to pay rent or salaries. Businesses with very high LTV/CAC, which can range from 5 to more than 20, pay relatively little to acquire future gross profits from customers.

Customer acquisition payback period (CAPB): CAPB is a gauge for how aggressive a company can be in marketing and selling its services. To calculate the payback period, divide the total cost of customer acquisition by the gross margin generated from one customer. For example, if a company charges $50 per month for an exercise video product, at 80 percent gross margin, and the cost of customer acquisition is $150, then the payback period is equal to 150 / (80% × 50), or 3.75 months. The longer the payback period, the greater the risk that a customer churns and the marketing dollars paid to acquire the customer are lost, and vice versa.

Sales efficiency: Sales efficiency answers the question "If I invest $1 of sales and marketing this period, how much gross margin or revenue will I generate in the next period?" It's useful to understand the capital needs of the business and how much cash it will take to grow.

Index

Page references in *italics* refer to figures.